For my PFFs

Write Some Cool
SH!T

366 PROMPTS TO REKINDLE YOUR CREATIVITY

Anne Marie Wells

Star Belt
* * * *
PRESS

Text and creative design by Anne Marie Wells
Book cover design by Anne Marie Wells via Canva.com
Emojis designed by OpenMoji – the open-source emoji and icon project. License: CC BY-SA 4.0
Headshot by Mark Duggan

ISBN: 979-8-9994801-1-8

Disclaimer: Historical events, cultural references, quotes, and other references were fact checked to the best of the author's ability. Details in some personal anecdotes have been changed to protect identities. It is not the author's intention for this book of writing prompts to be used as a cited reference for facts or investigative journalism or anything other than entertainment. In all cases, the author attempted to be as politically correct and culturally sensitive as possible. If any of the references in this collection are incorrect or inappropriate, you can contact the author directly through her website. Please consider all mistakes as examples of Hanlon's Razor.

Dear Writer,

Let's start out right away by saying, as long as it's not for evil, there's no wrong way to use this book. If you dive in head first on New Year's Day and diligently complete each writing prompt through December 31st (even Leap Day on a non-Leap Year), that is great. If you flip through the pages once in a while and read a prompt for inspiration, also great. If you skim through the book and write nothing at all, no problem. If you tear out the pages and use them to potty train your puppy, that is your prerogative. There is no wrong way.

I'm mostly a poet and memoirist, so poetry and memoir tend to influence everything I do including writing this book. But I don't think you need to be a poet or memoirist to use this book. When a prompt invites you to "Write about something you carry with you," for example, it can easily be transmuted to "Write about something your protagonist/antagonist/whoever carries with them". *Or* if you are a visual artist, "*Draw/ Paint/Create* something you carry with you". There is no wrong way.

These prompts are here to spark creativity, yes, but also to encourage exploration, experimentation, and stepping outside your comfort zone. If you read a prompt and it inspires creation outside of the boundaries of the prompt itself, awesome! You could also just read them as entertainment, or they could sit on your shelf keeping your other unread books company. Whatever! There is no wrong way.

If and when you create something thanks to one or more of these prompts, I'd love to know! If you post it to social media, tag me. If you're not a social media person, shoot me an email through my website. I love receiving messages that are not creepy or mean, and if a message is not creepy or mean, I will more than likely respond.

Hey, and another thing... Thanks for getting this book. As a small-time indie author, your support helps me pay the rent and allows me to occasionally add guacamole to my burrito for an extra $2.99. From the bottom of my heart (which is technically called the apex), thank you, thank you, thank you.

Okay, one last thing... If you loved this book, please tell everyone you know (and even people you don't know) that you loved it. Pop your review up on any of those websites with book reviews, create a post on your socials telling your followers about it, or simply recommend it to a friend. One little #BookRec can really make an impact.

Ok TL;DR, there's no wrong way, I love you for getting this book, and thank you!

Love,

Anne Marie

P.S.

Access references, extra reading materials, personal photos, and more bonus content that go along with each prompt by scanning this QR code with your smartphone or other device. Or, you can visit...

AnneMarieWellsWriter.com/366bonus

Enjoy!

January 1

Happy New Year! Approximately 30-40% of Americans make New Year's resolutions—that's over one hundred million people! However, research suggests, only about 19% end up keeping their resolutions, and nearly half give up by the end of January.

So this year, I encourage you to BE A QUITTER! That's right, be a quitter! Not achieving a New Year's resolution can cause unnecessary shame, self-deprecation, and/or self-loathing. Who needs that? Not you!

Instead of writing about what you would like to resolve to do this year, write about untethering yourself from New Year's resolutions.

January 2

Unclear if it's the same people who make New Year's resolutions each year, but approximately 25% of legal-aged American adults will participate in "Dry January"—the commitment to not drink alcohol for the entire month.

Though this trend gained national traction in the US in the 2010s, it actually has its roots in 1940s Finland! During World War II, the Finnish government called on their soldiers and citizens to participate in "Raitis Tammikuu" or Sober January in an effort to conserve money and national resources as they resisted Soviet forces.

Write a Dear John letter to the cocktail (or non-alcoholic beverage!) of your choice.

January 3

Inspired by Kim Liao's *Lit Hub* article "Why You Should Aim For 100 Rejections a Year", writer Reneé Bibby started the annual Rejection Competition. This free, easygoing contest tracks which participants receive the most literary rejections within a calendar year. She even created multiple divisions of "Rejecterinos" to level the playing fields for those who submit their work for publication a lot versus those who don't submit as much or who are new to the submission process.

I know, personally, while participating in the competition, whenever I received a rejection, the sting was mitigated by the satisfaction of adding it to my tally on the contest sheet.

Today, get behind the steering wheel of rejection. Write a rejection letter to yourself or someone else. (You probably don't want to send it though!)

January 4

A parable found in David Bayles and Ted Orland's book *Art & Fear* recounts the story of a ceramics teacher who divided their class into two groups. One group was instructed to create the most perfect pot they possibly could. The second group was instructed to make as many pots as they could without focusing on perfection. The result? The first group, so hung up on creating their absolute best work, spent all their time planning out their pots of perfection that they ended up making nothing at all. The second group, on the other hand, made lots of mistakes, but then learned and improved their skills as they made pot after pot. Their pots ended up being of higher quality and more inventive, and they had a lot more of them to boot!

Today, write as many ideas for stories or poems or creations as you can. Aim for 100 total ideas. It doesn't matter if some of them are boring or cliché. Just aim for 100. If you can come up with even more than that, then even better!

January 5

Simon Berger is a visual artist from Switzerland. He creates his masterpieces by hitting glass with a hammer! No, he doesn't shatter the glass. Instead, he makes very precise decisions about location and force in order to create ghostly portraits. His broken glass art has been exhibited all over the world even though he has said in a feature with 60 Second Docs that "mostly things don't go according to plan."

Write about a time something did not go according to plan. Even if things didn't turn out well at the time, the story of the debacle can live a new life in the form of creative writing.

January 6

The Great Pacific Garbage Patch is a 620,000 sq. mi. (1.6M sq. km.) mass in the Pacific Ocean composed almost entirely of plastic waste. It's twice the size of Texas and three times the size of France. But it didn't just appear. The patch formed over decades as trash was either intentionally or accidentally discarded in waterways and then trapped in the vortex created by the ocean's water and wind currents.

Yet, some animals continue to persist in this "plastisphere". Animals that normally thrive on coastlines are finding an unlikely home away from home, living among open-ocean species by using the plastic as a substitute for solid ground.

Cue Oscar the Grouch: ♫ *I love trash* ♫

Today, write something *trashy* whatever that means to you.

January 7

One of the works created by artists Michael Dumontier and Neil Farber depict a panda in a small boat with a turtle on its back. Above the duo are the words "Friends don't have to make sense."

Is there a person in your life who is completely different from you, but whom you adore? Write about your differences, how these differences appear to others, and how these differences appear to one another.

January 8

In Susan Cain's nonfiction book, *Bittersweet: How Sorrow and Longing Make Us Whole*, which explores the interconnectedness of our complex emotions and how joy and sorrow are often experienced together, she describes attending a conference in Portugal where she was given an atypical fortune cookie. It was called a "sadness cookie," and the message inside her cookie read, "Those who let their eyes adjust can see in the darkness."

Write about what you might see in the metaphorical or literal darkness if you let your eyes adjust. What do you wish you could see (whether real or imaginary) if your eyes could adjust enough?

January 9

Whale sharks have the thickest skin of any other known animal, measuring in at 4-6 inches (10-15 centimeters) thick. The thick skin, which more resembles rubber than skin, defends the creature from spears and arrows as well as predators that bite—like other sharks! Its skin is also covered in a layer of mucus which protects the animal from bacteria and parasites. The very thick skin and the very thin layer of mucus each perform an important role in the creature's life.

Write about two things that are very different in size or traits, but that serve equally important roles in your life.

January 10

Kurt Halsey Frederiksen is a contemporary American pop artist who has since retreated into obscurity. His works feature mostly poignant but sometimes silly depictions of animals and people often accompanied by short phrases that called to my teenaged, emo heart like, "We are more than most will ever find" and "there are far worse things to regret…"

Many theories exist for why he stopped creating and discontinued his website, but which rumors are true (or close to true) and which ones are merely speculation? Probably only Frederiksen knows for certain.

In today's writing, explore where you might go or who you might become if you wanted to disappear from your current life and start over.

January 11

A "zeitgeber" is any external or environmental cue that influences an organism's biological rhythms. For example, the shift in daylight hours and temperature cues certain species of trees to either drop their leaves and become dormant for autumn and winter, or start budding their leaves and waking up for spring and summer.

I propose the concept of "social zeitgbers" or external cues created by our society that inform our social rhythms—behaviors, routines, and traditions. For example, changes in weather may influence what foods we eat like when we eat soup in winter or ice cream in the summer. The social zeitgeber of school starting in the fall might alter our commutes to work or alter what time we get up in the morning so that our kiddos make it to the bus on time.

Write about the zeitgebers, whether natural or socially created, that influence your everyday life.

January 12

Today's prompt is a two-parter. As challenging as it is, try not to look ahead so the result of the prompt is as authentic as possible.

Recall an event that changed your life whether positively or negatively. (In fact, negatively might work better if you're willing to go there!) Imagine the scene as if it were a movie and then freeze on a single frame of the film. Describe the scene in front of you from top to bottom, from sky (or ceiling) to ground, as if you were describing a painting. Think also of the senses that might not come across in a painting—such as the sounds or smells—taking place in the scene.

Save this writing and use it as the foundation for a prompt found later on in this book.

January 13

When scientists first studied a certain species of anglerfish in the 1800s, they realized all of their collected and observed specimens were female. The phenomenon puzzled researchers for over a century. Where were all the males?

Well, in the early 1900s, the minuscule males were observed attaching themselves to the much larger females. Once latched, the male would become fully dependent on the female for nutrients, and over time lose the organs needed for seeing, swimming, and eating. The two fish would more or less become one organism, with the male only providing sperm whenever the female was ready to spawn. How romantic!

Write about the ways in which you atrophied as a result of a relationship. Have you been able to regrow since? Why or why not?

January 14

In mid-January 1995, wolves were reintroduced to Yellowstone National Park, and the subsequent changes observed were unanticipated. Grazers who historically had no predators in the area began to disperse and move more around the land instead of staying in one place. Because the grass by waterways wasn't overgrazed, the soil started to firm up, preventing erosion. Because the water wasn't full of eroded sediment, beavers and fish populations returned. The saplings that would be munched on right away by grazers had a chance to grow into mature willows and cottonwoods, providing habitat for songbirds and migratory species. Even though the wolves weren't decimating the grazer populations, just their presence altered the grazers' behavior, leading to incredible restoration to the Greater Yellowstone Ecosystem.

Write about how the introduction or re-introduction of an entity in your life resulted in incredible restoration.

January 15

Every Saturday in Sweden, one can expect to find individuals and families buying mix-and-match candy from local candy shops. The tradition known as "Lördagsgodis" or "Saturday Candy" began in the mid-20th century when health experts saw a rise in tooth decay as national incomes increased and more and more individuals could afford to buy sweet indulgences more regularly. As a result, they encouraged limiting sugar intake to just once a week. Now "Saturday Candy" is less about abating cavities and more about the value of money. Children learn how to save their coins in order to purchase something they really want.

Write about a "Saturday Candy" equivalent in your own life. Is there something you indulge in once a week? Maybe it's a food item, or maybe it's sleeping late, watching a certain TV show, or other indulgence.

January 16

In Rudy Francisco's poem "And Then After" from his collection *Helium*, the speaker describes a story they once heard about a Palestinian woman who would convert used teargas grenades into flower pots. Francisco concludes the poem with, "From this I learned / the explosion // is not how the story / has to end."

For today's prompt, imagine how a weapon or item whose main purpose is violence could be upcycled into an object of peace or even into a mundane household item. What alterations might this object have to undergo to reach its more enlightened self?

January 17

While speaking to the schoolgirls of Elizabeth Garrett Anderson School in Islington, north London, United Kingdom, Michelle Obama recounted that she was "an example of what is possible when girls from the very beginning of their lives are loved and nurtured by people around them." She went on to say, "I was surrounded by extraordinary women in my life who taught me about quiet strength and dignity."

In today's writing, include someone who displays "quiet strength." Describe how they demonstrate this quality.

January 18

Before the continents existed in the way we know them today, two-thirds of Earth's landmass fit together like puzzle pieces to form the supercontinent Gondwana. In the 1980s, researchers discovered a set of dinosaur footprints embedded in mud and silt in Cameroon. Four decades later, in 2024, matching footprints were found in Brazil confirming that dinosaurs existed in a region that now makes up South America and Africa before the continents split apart 120 million years ago.

In today's writing, include a set of footprints. Who do they belong to? Is there just one set? Multiple sets? Where are they heading? Where did they come from? What shoes are they wearing, if any? Why?

January 19

Inspired by her father who struggled with illiteracy into adulthood, in 1995 acclaimed country and pop singer Dolly Parton started a program that provided free books to children from birth to age five. She called it The Imagination Library. The program started in her home county of Sevier, Tennessee and expanded over time to communities all over the USA, Canada, the UK, Australia, and Ireland. As of this writing, the program has given away almost 300 million books.

Did you have a favorite book or story as a child? Write about its effect on you. What was it about the story or the illustrations that piqued your interest? Or, if no book or story stands out to you, write about a story that means a lot to you now.

January 20

Today, revisit the two-part prompt from January 12th. If you're bouncing around the journal instead of executing each prompt one by one chronologically, then you might want to go back to the 12th to set the foundation for today's prompt.

Self-help guru and "Father of Motivation," Dr. Wayne W. Dyer made popular the quote attributed to Nobel Prize-winning quantum physicist Max Planck, "Change the way you look at things and the things you look at change."

Using this quote as inspiration, look at your previous writing from a new perspective. How might the scene change if it were described by a drill sergeant? A yoga instructor? Someone who loves you unconditionally? Someone who hates you unconditionally? Someone who doesn't know you at all? Someone who grew up in the arctic tundra? Someone who grew up in foster care? A motorcycle enthusiast? Chess champion?

January 21

The sun is about 93 million miles (150 million kilometers) away from Earth. The light emitted from the sun takes about eight minutes and twenty seconds to reach Earth's surface. Often the light doesn't meet the ground because it is obstructed by a tree, a house, a mountain, a human being, or something else, creating a shadow on the ground in place of the light.

Write from the perspective of the light. How would you feel to travel all that way just to be blocked? Do you resent not reaching the ground? Are you grateful? What might you say to the object blocking your path? What might you say to the shadow created in your absence?

January 22

According to the World Economic Forum, more people aged 100 or older are alive in the world than ever before. Even so, reaching 100 years old is still a very rare feat. Japan has the highest percentage of centenarians at about 0.06% of their population and the United States has the highest number of centenarians at about 97,000 total.

Imagine the year in which you will turn 100. Write about how the world will be different. What do you regularly do today that will be completely different in the year you turn 100? Who will be the leader of your country? How will you communicate with others? How will you go from place to place?

January 23

"To postpone" means to arrange for an event to take place at a later time than it was originally scheduled. To me, the most obvious opposite of "*post*pone" would be "*pre*pone", meaning to take place at an earlier time than originally scheduled, but this word only exists in common usage in Indian English; it isn't used or accepted as a word anywhere else outside of the subcontinent. (In fact, right now my word processor is underlining it in red, indicating an error.) Why is that, though? It makes perfect sense, and there is no other word that fully encapsulates the meaning of "prepone." Some suggestions for antonyms to "postpone" from Thesaurus.com include "expedite" and "hasten" which don't quite capture the same essence.

Write about the ways in which a country, community, or culture outside your own gets something right. How does this element compare to what you are used to?

January 24

Today, experiment with a piece of writing. If it's written in the first-person "I" point-of-view, change it (or an excerpt of it) to be written in the third-person "he/she/they" point-of-view. Change it again to the second-person "you" point-of-view. How did this change how the piece reads or how you interact with it?

Now, if it's written in present tense, change it so it's written in past tense (or vice versa). How did this change the impact of the piece this time?

Then change it back to its original version. Did you discover anything new? If yes, great. If not, also great.

January 25

REM is the stage during which most dreaming occurs. Both historically and today, people believe dreams connect us with the spiritual world. REM has been documented in species across the animal kingdom including dogs, lizards, octopuses, birds, fish, and even spiders! But researchers still don't have a definitive answer as to why dreaming would be advantageous in the course of evolution. Some theorists believe dreaming allows us to rehearse emotions and behaviors in different contexts. Others believe it might be a side effect as waste and toxins flush out of the brain through cerebrospinal fluid. Or, it might be a way for the subconscious psyche to express itself.

Write about a dream you still remember having. Whether it be a nightmare or a nonsensical dream, write as much as you can remember, then allow your stream of consciousness to follow. Maybe you fill in the blanks the dream left behind. Maybe you analyze what the dream represents on a metaphorical level. Or maybe your pen takes you somewhere else. Go with the flow.

January 26

When I was 25, while backpacking The Florida National Scenic Trail, I came upon a Hare Krishna guru who read my palm in exchange for some leopard print duct tape. He told me after traveling the world, I would marry a man at least ten years older than I was and make his home my home. And it happened! Though we met in Wyoming where we were both living at the time, I coincidentally moved to the area where my now-husband (who is more than ten years older than I am) originally grew up. After a long-distance relationship, he eventually relocated and we settled not far to where his family still lives.

Whether it came true or not, write about a prediction either you or someone else had about your or someone else's future.

January 27

In addition to predicting the dynamic of my future romantic relationship, the Hare Krishna guru who read my palm when I was 25 that I mentioned yesterday also told me that in one of my past lives I was a Norwegian mountaineer who succumbed to the elements.

Whether you believe in past lives or not, imagine who you might have been in a past era. Who might you have been if you had lived in Chicago at the turn of the 20th century, or Japan in the year 827, or the Roman Republic in 400 BCE?

January 28

Studies have shown that exercising stimulates the synthesis of myokines, a kind of protein that reduces inflammation in the body. These proteins can decrease feelings of stress and depression and have been nicknamed "hope molecules."

Today, write only after having moved your body in some way, whether it's a walk or a seated dance party. If you're not able to move your body, myokines can also be produced from massage. Write in a stream of consciousness post-myokine release.

January 29

In American author Elizabeth Gilbert's book *Big Magic*, she describes the writing strategy of dressing up for the muse. She recounts examples of writers wearing a particular suit coat or color lipstick in order to attract the muse and inspire one's creativity.

Let's try it today! Don that item that sits in the closet but never gets worn. Maybe it's a tuxedo or ball gown. Maybe it's a certain pair of high heels or an interesting hat. Or maybe you live in Texas but own a ski suit. Maybe you own snorkel gear that has gone unused. How about that vampire costume from years ago? Now is the time to brush the dust off. Once you're in your get up, get writing. Does your outfit influence your writing style or tone?

January 30

Grip strength, believe it or not, is one of the best predictors of longevity. Besides the fact that people with greater grip strength tend to be more active, older adults with solid grip strength are more likely to catch themselves before falling. However, our modern lifestyle—the way we use smartphones and computers—has made human hands weaker overall. But never fear, according to physical therapists, an easy way to improve grip strength is by practicing the "farmer's carry," or carrying equally weighted objects in either hand, like when carrying groceries home from the store.

Write about something you carry with you. Is it a tangible object or a memory or metaphor? Does it work to strengthen you or weaken you?

January 31

"Code-switching" describes when an individual uses different languages or different methods of speaking in different settings typically to avoid conflict or to better fit in with social expectations. For example, a person might use a different accent or dialect or put on their "customer service voice" while working their corporate job, which is completely different from how they would speak if they were reading a story to a child or attending a birthday party with friends. Or, someone might normally speak using a lot of F-bombs, but then never swear in front of their mother or in their place of worship.

Write about the ways in which you code-switch throughout your day-to-day life. How do certain words come out differently? What happens to your tone of voice in different situations? What colloquialisms or accents emerge in different settings? Can all these different voices appear in your writing somehow?

February 1

Carter G. Woodson is attributed with setting the foundations that led to National Black History Month. In American history, he is the only person whose parents had been enslaved to earn a PhD degree, having earned his doctorate in history from Harvard University in 1912. He went on to found the Association for the Study of Negro Life and History (which later became the Association for the Study of African American Life and History) and initiated Negro History Week on February 7, 1926, choosing this week because Black Americans had already been observing Abraham Lincoln and Fredrick Douglass' birthdays on February 12th and 14th, respectively. It wouldn't be until more than two decades after his death in 1950 that National Black History Month would be recognized by the US government.

Write about Black History Month's impact in your own life. What are your earliest memories of the observance? Are there ways you have observed this tradition or would like to this year or in the future?

February 2

An acronym is a set of letters that represent the first letters in a set of words and that is pronounced as its own word. For example NASA (pronounced NA-suh) is the acronym for National Aeronautics and Space Administration.

A *backronym*, on the other hand, starts with the acronymic letters first, and then fills in the corresponding words afterward. For example, AMBER alerts that are sent to cell phones and through TV broadcasts to announce when a child has gone missing was originally named after a little girl who was abducted in 1996. Later, it was announced that AMBER would stand for America's Missing: Broadcast Emergency Response.

In today's writing, include a backronym. Maybe it's the letters in your name. Or maybe you turn a common household item into a backronym. LAMP: Light that Amplifies My Perception.

February 3

In the world that fantasy author Patrick Rothfuss created in his novel *The Wise Man's Fear*, a famous philosopher named Teccam is credited with the quote, "There are three things all wise men fear: the sea in storm, a night with no moon, and the anger of a gentle man."

Write about to what extent this proverb speaks to your lived experience.

February 4

In the mid-1990s about half a million human deaths in India were attributed to vultures. No, vultures didn't attack humans. Rather, the population of over 50 million vultures dropped an estimated 95-99% because of a medicine used to treat sick cows. The medicine would linger in the cows' carcasses, and when the vultures feasted on the dead animals, the medicine entered the vultures' bodies causing kidney failure. As a result of the decimation in the vulture population, pathogens from rotting animals became more prolific and spread more easily within human communities.

Write about an event that should have been positive but caused unintended negative effects.

February 5

Believe it or not, until February 2024, the state of Nebraska's tourism slogan was, "Nebraska, honestly it's not for everyone."

Write the reasons why your home state or region isn't for everyone. Is it even for you? What would help a local or visitor appreciate it more?

February 6

Each year since his death on February 6, 2020, I adorn barren graves with flowers to pay homage to my father. For many years, my father was the caretaker for the cemetery where his parents were buried in Upstate New York. He was not compensated for this work at all, but did it merely so that his parents, and those who were buried there, would have some dignity in their resting place. He even went so far as to purchase a riding lawn mower with his own money just to take care of the cemetery. But my father was also very humble about his efforts. I didn't even learn that he purchased a riding lawnmower until after he passed away. (If you read my book *Survived By*, you might recognize this story from my poem "Gravestone Flowers".)

Write about the ways in which you honor your dead.

February 7

Though it doesn't look like it, coral that make up coral reefs are actually *animals!* Each individual is called a coral polyp and measures one to three millimeters in diameter. As larvae, they attach themselves to hard surfaces like rocks and then build up over time. In fact, the Great Barrier Reef off the eastern coast of Australia, is the largest structure in the world that was built by living creatures, measuring about 134,000 square miles (347,000 square kilometers)!

Finding inspiration from the wee coral polyp, write about what you would like to see in your life build up over time like a coral reef. What would you *not* like to see build up over time?

February 8

On more than one occasion at locations across the globe, zoos have gone to great lengths to fool patrons into believing certain animals were on the premises when they in fact were not. The Houston Zoo admitted to posing rubber snakes in terrariums, and the Taizhou Zoo in China went as far as painting chow chows and claiming they were pandas.

Write about feeling like an imposter. When have you felt the most like a rubber snake or chow chow in disguise?

February 9

Scientists estimate that there are 20 quadrillion ants on Earth (about 2.5 million ants per person!) Before the industrialization of yogurt-making using lab-made starters (or blends of bacteria that cause milk to ferment into yogurt), traditional yogurt-making processes in Turkey and Bulgaria used ants! They would place a few ants in a cup of milk, and the microbes that were naturally occurring on the ants' bodies along with the ants' formic acid as well as proteases (enzymes that breakdown protein) created by the ants would kickstart the fermentation process. Some communities are trying to bring back these forgotten practices and have experimented with different species of ants to find the one that makes the best yogurt!

Write about what ingredients you need in order to create your best writing. What is your metaphorical equivalent to ants? What kickstarts you into writing? Is there a way you can harness its power?

February 10

Onomatopoeia is a word created as a description of a sound associated with it. For example "cluck," "chirp," "meow," and "moo" are all onomatopoeias. Besides animal sounds, many words in the English language originated as onomatopoeia, even adopting the onomatopoeias of other languages. For example, the word cliché is an onomatopoeia derived from the French. It was used to describe the sound a printing press makes when ink is stamped to paper. The word bamboo derived from the tropics, likely from Malay. Because of its hollow core, when bamboo is put in a fire, it explodes. Bamboo!

Close your eyes and listen to the sounds around you. Try to derail your brain from the descriptive words you're used to. For example, instead of describing the hot kettle as whistling, maybe you describe it as rooing. Instead of the sink dripping, maybe the sink blets. When you've invented at least one onomatopoeia, incorporate it into a piece of writing.

February 11

My father was born on this day in 1945. He lived to be 74 and 360 days, dying only five days before his 75th birthday from a short battle with lung cancer. Before his illness halted his life, my father was known for his intentional and random acts of kindness. Ever since I was a child, he had the habit of going on long walks at night, sometimes not coming home until midnight or later, either walking the family dog, or walking laps around the track near our house. When my parents moved to Florida, he'd take long walks around the winding culs-de-sac in their neighborhood. Their HOA mandated that all homes must have their light posts functioning at all times; if someone's light post was out, they'd be cited. My dad started changing the bulbs for the houses he noticed had burnt out light posts. Because it happened so often, he began carrying light bulbs in his pockets as he made his rounds at night, just in case.

Write about a stranger's act of kindness—large or small—that had an impact on your life.

February 12

Even though they don't fit the archetype one would expect, sharks and stingrays are species of fish! These unique animals are born from "mermaid purses," which are dark, leathery egg cases that kind of look like little pillows with a hook in each corner. Sometimes you can find them washed up on a beach.

In today's writing, include some merfolk. Bonus points if they have purses with interesting gizmos and whatsits and thingamabobs inside.

February 13

The oldest known map in the world as of this writing, was found etched into a mammoth tusk in the Czech Republic, and is estimated to date back to 25,000 BCE. Archaeologists believe the map was likely used while hunting.

Today, write some creative directions to somewhere. Maybe your directions describe how to get to a fictitious place or maybe they're directions to your favorite restaurant. They can literally list which turns and roads to take, or they can be more figurative. Bonus points for drawing a map with your writing.

February 14

It's Valentine's Day! What better way to observe the holiday than to ruminate on our breakups?

The Museum of Broken Relationships located in Zagreb, Croatia, exhibits personal objects like photographs, letters, and keepsakes left over from former lovers. The collection began after two Croatian artists ended their four-year relationship and joked about exhibiting nostalgic items in a museum. They amassed hundreds of anonymous donations and the exhibition has now toured all over the globe.

Write about the items that would be exhibited in your own Museum of Broken Relationships. What would be included in their annotations? The dates and locations of the relationship? The material the object is made out of? Would there be an Artist Statement?

February 15

A "red herring" is a plot device used often in mystery writing and is meant to mislead a reader into believing something false about a situation—usually about the true identity of the story's culprit and/or their motive.

The plot device is so named because when preserving herring through salting and smoking, it turns red and gives off a strong, pungent smell. The smell is so strong that it can distract and divert hunting dogs from whatever scent they are tracking.

Include a red herring in a piece of writing whether new or previously written. Think about what you want your reader to believe, and what might cause them to reconsider those beliefs.

February 16

If you've ever been at any kind of group orientation or introductory meeting, you may have engaged in the icebreaker activity called "Two Truths and a Lie" during which participants share three statements without disclosing which are true and which one is false. The rest of the participants then try to guess which statement is the lie.

Today in your writing, incorporate two truths and a lie without disclosing which is which.

February 17

Though we didn't start dating until my sophomore year, my high school boyfriend and I met in karate class when we were in middle school. I have a distinct memory of climbing trees together at an overnight karate camp and him asking me to be his girlfriend... I said no!

We broke up in high school as most high school couples do, and we tried dating again later in our twenties. Despite our romantic attempts not working out, we have kept in touch over the years. We both married other people, but still catch up once in a while and stay in contact on social media.

Write the story of your high school sweetheart or other relationship—whether romantic or platonic—you had from high school.

February 18

In his novel *Zorba the Greek,* 20th-century Greek author Nikos Kazantzakis, wrote "Everything in the world has a hidden meaning... Men, animals, trees, stars, they are all hieroglyphics. When you see them you do not understand them. You think they are really men, animals, trees, stars. It is only years later that you understand."

In today's writing, include a hidden meaning. Maybe the hidden meaning lies within something exciting, like a lion, a sparkly dress, or the city of Los Angeles. Or maybe the hidden meaning lies within something prosaic—an hour-long commute, instant oatmeal, a reality TV show, a sneaker, a stapler, a piece of toilet paper, or other humdrum object.

February 19

Occam's Razor, attributed to 14th century philosopher William of Occam (or Ockham), is a principle that maintains that the simplest explanation is usually the most accurate.

In a similar vein, the phrase "When you hear hoofbeats, think horses, not zebras" is commonly used in medical diagnoses when presented with a list of symptoms, suggesting that the most likely possibility should be considered before rarer possibilities.

Today, write the most cockamamie explanation for something mundane. There's a knock at the door, who or what is causing the sound? A store's door is locked even though there's an open sign in the window. How come? Be as outlandish as you can.

February 20

William of Occam is not the only person with a famous razor. Author Robert J. Hanlon is attributed with Hanlon's Razor, or the rule of thumb that "one should not attribute malice to something that can be explained by stupidity." In other words, give people the benefit of the doubt. They're probably not an a-hole, they're probably just an idiot.

Write about a situation in which one or more person's failings can be attributed to their lack of intelligence rather than an abundance of malevolence.

February 21

I knew my husband was "the one" when we went snow-shoeing together for the first time. Not a mile into our excursion, I developed a blister on my foot. I tried to play it cool, but I knew with more mileage ahead of us, I was going to suffer the rest of the way. When I finally confessed to my discomfort, instead of turning around and heading home, he plodded off the trail and pulled a *folded avalanche shovel* from his backpack. He made a little trench in the snow for us to sit in, and then pulled out his first aid kit. I took off my boot and sock, and he kept my foot warm under his long johns. As he fashioned the perfect blister bandage from some medical tape and a piece of foam he cut out in the shape of a donut, I sipped hot cocoa from his thermos and fell even more wildly in love. He was so *prepared* and so *thoughtful.* *swoon*

Write about how you knew your partner was "the one," or if you're flying solo, write about how you *would* know someone was the right person for you either romantically or as a friend. Imagine what they would say or do that would demonstrate this.

February 22

If I could go back in time to pursue any career I wanted, I would have become a professional wrestler with World Wrestling Entertainment (aka The WWE). The tacky outfits, the gymnastics, the hammy theatrical displays? Ugh! I truly missed my calling. I've joked many times that someday I will encourage my son to become a professional wrestler. I came up with a whole schtick. His alias would be "Mama's Boy" and I would act as his "manager." Then during the final tag-team match when his tag teammate is somehow injured, and it looks like they're going to lose the championship, he would go against the rules and tag me in, and then I, Mama's Boy's Mama would defeat the opposing team by doing my signature move: "putting them to bed."

Write about your dream profession no matter how absurd. What would you wear? Who would you work with? What would your goals be? Imagine a conversation between you and another person that might take place while working this dream job.

February 23

In 2021 two hundred coffins fell from a cliff-side cemetery in Camogli, Italy into the Ligurian sea after a landslide. As the city government worked on recovering the coffins, dozens of citizens gathered in front of the town hall waiting to hear news of whether or not their ancestors' remains had been found.

Write from the perspective of one of the ancestors whose coffin fell into the sea. What would you want your living relatives to know?

February 24

Every year in mid- to late-February, Yosemite National Park in California experiences the miraculous "Firefall" when the usually "unremarkable" Horsetail Falls is hit just right by the setting sun. For this once-a-year phenomenon to happen, the sky needs to be clear, the sun needs to hit the falls at the perfect angle, and the falls need to have enough water in them to reflect the sun. The result is a few minutes of an ethereal molten orange cascade.

Write about a transformation you make once-a-year. Do you go on vacation and transform into a world traveler? Do you attend a special event that requires getting dressed up? What is your equivalent of transforming into an ethereal molten orange cascade?

February 25

As of this writing, fewer than two dozen people have earned an EGOT—an Emmy, Grammy, Oscar, and Tony award. Among those, Robert Lopez—the mastermind behind the hit songs of Disney's *Frozen* and *Coco* movies as well as co-creator of the Broadway hits *The Book of Mormon* and *Avenue Q*—not only earned the distinction, he was the first person to earn it *twice*. When he first achieved the EGOT at age 39, he was the youngest person to have done so and also set the record for fastest time span of earning one: just ten years. The second time he earned the EGOT, he broke his own record, paring down the time he took to earn it to just seven years.

Which personal record would you like to break? The fastest time to write a chapter? Or the most pages you ever wrote in one go? Beyond writing, perhaps you'd like to break your record for the longest time you've gone without checking your email or how much Greek yogurt you've consumed in one sitting. Whether silly or serious, try to break a record and use that experience to inspire your writing.

February 26

One of my favorite flavors is coconut. I go gaga for coconut cake, coconut candy, coconut donuts. I love it all. My mom and sister, on the other hand, both hate it. Lucky for me, whenever there's a box of chocolates around, like during the holidays, they pass all the coconut flavored ones to me. Yum!

Write about a flavor or flavor combination you love that is unique or just might not be the most popular. Describe it in detail. How did you discover it? Write about a time this flavor was particularly significant to you.

February 27

In the early 2000s, Stacy London and Clinton Kelly, hosted the reality series *What Not to Wear*, in which guests were nominated by their loved ones to have a makeover. The hosts would trash the guest's fashion choices before sending them off into New York City with $5,000 to buy new clothes that met certain criteria of what the duo deemed to be appropriate for their age, body type, and/or profession. At the end of the show, the guest would reveal their new look to those who nominated them.

A decade later, the hosting duo ditched their fashion judgment in a new show called *Wear Whatever the F You Want*. The premise was to help guests who felt stuck in fashion ruts make their fashion dreams come true. Guests included a goth who wanted a preppy makeover and a former Amish woman who wanted to dress like Dolly Parton. (My dream style is circus clown meets elegant old lady; lots of bright colors and sparkle.)

Write about how you would dress if money and societal expectations weren't factors.

February 28

Kehinde Wiley is a portraitist famous for painting modernly-dressed Black protagonists in poses and backgrounds that reference centuries-old works. For example, his painting "Napoleon Leading the Army over the Alps" which portrays a young Black man in army fatigues, white t-shirt, and bandana draped in a flowing golden fabric atop a rearing white horse was inspired by Jacques-Louis David's painting from the 1800s, "Napoleon Crossing the Alps" which depicts the famous French military leader in the same pose.

In today's writing, find inspiration from a work that is considered a "classic". Recreate it with modern parallels whether those be in language, imagery, or other elements.

February 29

Is it Leap Year this year? If not, you can either skip this day or complete the prompt as a bonus. Reader's choice!

Only about .06% of the world population is a "leapling," a person born on Leap Day. As expected, February 29th is the rarest birthday with only a 1 in 1,460 chance of being born on this day. The most famous leapling is actually a fictional character: Superman!

Write yourself into a superhero. What are your super powers? What is your superhero name? And what is your origin story? Do you have an arch-nemesis? How do you keep your identity secret? Or don't you? Let your ideas take you up, up, and away!

March 1

The month of March's etymology stems from the Roman god of war, Mars. In Ancient Rome, March was considered the first month of the year and would typically be the time when the military would be re-engaged in war campaigns after the winter.

Write about what you'd like to start being re-engaged in after these last winter months.

March 2

The term "ikigai" is derived from the Japanese philosophy meaning "life worth". Ikigai is often explained using a four-circle Venn diagram. One circle represents what brings enjoyment, another represents what one is skilled at, another represents what one is paid to do, and the last represents what the world needs.

Is writing your ikigai? If not, what is? What do you want to be your ikigai? After you've determined what your ikigai is or what you want it to be, write about how it fits into each of the four circles. Is your Venn diagram lopsided? How might you correct it so that your ikigai is in balance?

March 3

In the Tanakh or Old Testament of the Christian Bible, God is referred to as YHWH (often anglicized to Yahweh). Some believe the four-letter tetragrammaton is derived from a verb meaning "to be" or "to cause to become," or "I am who I am." Some believe the letter combinations represent the sound of inhalation "YH" and the sound of exhalation "WH," meaning that God is breath, and therefore life.

Write about your breath. When has breathing felt easy? When has it felt difficult? In what ways does your breath parallel your life?

March 4

In Julia Cameron's book, *The Artist's Way*, she emphasizes the necessity to complete "morning pages" every day. During one's morning pages, a writer takes pen to paper (not fingers to keyboard) to hand write three full pages of stream of consciousness. She believes dumping out all of the wayward thoughts that crowd one's brain space helps to make room for higher quality creativity. Even if the writer simply repeats "I don't know what to write" over and over for three pages, she still believes there is great benefit from maintaining the practice.

Today (even if you have done so already!) write three pages of stream of consciousness, even if you only write "I don't know what to write" over and over again.

March 5

Lisa Gautier is the president of the nonprofit organization Matter of Trust which most notably uses human hair to clean up oil spills. Human hair is capable of holding up to seven times its weight in oil. Utilizing this knowledge, Gautier and her team set out to create mats made of human hair that can be used to clean up oil spills. The program has become so popular that she has had to expand their efforts to satellite locations, loaning out equipment and guiding other groups in creating human hair mats to clean water contaminated by oil.

Write about an object that was given a new life with a completely different purpose.

March 6

Nonbinary author, poet, comedian, and activist, ALOK, whom I refer to as a modern sage, once said in an interview, "The work of authenticity actually is about [being authentic while] knowing that everyone around you is going to doubt you, is going to judge you, is going to try to pull you back into a version of yourself that you're not, is going to try to minimize you, is going to try to punish you, and to keep going anyways."

Write about the work you have done (or need to do) to be your most authentic self in the face of doubt, judgment, minimization, and/or punishment.

March 7

Déja vu is the phenomenon someone experiences when they feel like they have seen, heard, or otherwise already lived something occurring in the present time. A lesser-known phenomenon *jamais vu* is a phenomenon someone experiences when they feel as if they are seeing something they have regularly seen for the first time.

Write about something you're very familiar with as if you're seeing it/experiencing it for the first time. If you were a stranger, how would you describe your living space? If you were a foreigner, how would you describe your town? How would you describe your partner, friend, or family member if you had never met them before? Look at something or someone with brand new eyes.

March 8

While taking a nonfiction writing workshop with essayist Rachel Stevens, she recalled how when she and her partner were coming up with a name for their daughter, someone told them that a good way to make sure it was the perfect name was to imagine someone in the future wanting to set their friend up on a date with them. "Oh my God, you have to meet my friend _____."

Whether you're partnered already or not, write from the perspective of someone wanting to set you up with their friend. What would they say that would intrigue a stranger into sharing a meal or a round of putt-putt with you? Start by writing, "Oh my God, you have to meet my friend" and then insert your own name.

March 9

When I was growing up, maybe once a year, my mom would make fried dough for dinner. (We'd call it "pizza fritta" in our house.) No vegetables. No protein. Just some dough, fried up in some Crisco, and covered in cinnamon and sugar. It was such a huge deal. I loved when my mom would let me take the hot pieces of dough and shake them in a paper bag filled with the cinnamon sugar mixture. Even as a teenager, on this special day when the idea of a square meal was tossed out the window, I'd squeal and dance, singing ♫ *Pizza fritta for dinner! Pizza fritta for dinner!* ♫

Write about a treat you remember having as a kid.

March 10

Right around this time, many folks in the United States are "springing forward," adjusting their clocks into Daylight Savings Time. Whether you enjoy Daylight Savings Time or think its outdated, it makes me think of the aubade.

An aubade is a poem or song written about the early morning and typically laments leaving or being left by a lover. A great example is John Denver's "Leaving on a Jet Plane." However, aubades have evolved over time, and many have no inclusion of romance whatsoever.

In today's writing, use the rising sun as a symbol of an ending whether it be the ending of a romance, the ending of an era in one's life, or some other kind of ending. Then write a second version of the same writing, but this time make the rising sun a symbol of joy, hope, and/or a new beginning beaming with potential. Is there a way for these two versions to co-exist somehow?

March 11

In Douglas Adams' famed sci-fi series *The Hitchhiker's Guide to the Galaxy*, the answer to the "Ultimate Question of Life, the Universe, and Everything" is determined by a supercomputer to be 42. Though Adams said he chose the number arbitrarily, many fans sought a deeper meaning. Some theorize the number represents the average number of lines on a paperback book page. Others believe 42 represents unity because when light hits water at a 42° angle, it makes a rainbow. Others theorize 42 represents death because when pronouncing four and two in Japanese, they sound like the Japanese word for dying.

Adams affirmed multiple times he chose the number at random, leaving some to argue that the quest to make meaning and find an answer is even more powerful than the actual answer itself.

Today, write your own answer to the "Ultimate Question of Life, The Universe, and Everything" whatever you determine that question to be.

March 12

Famed physicist Albert Einstein once said, "[T]o regard old questions from new angles... requires creative imagination and makes real advances." What questions have you been ruminating on recently? Can you approach these old questions from new angles? What would it look like to swap the questioning word to a different one? For example, "*When* will there be peace on Earth?" might transform into "*Who* will bring peace on Earth?" or "*What* would peace on Earth look like?"

Transform your old question and answer it, even if you don't actually know the answer. Suppose. Hypothesize. Or completely make it up and write a bunch of bull sh!t.

March 13

In many cultures around the world, the monthly full moons throughout the year have held special names based on natural or cultural events that happen around their viewing in the sky. For example, some southern Native American tribes would refer to the full moon in March as the Worm Moon because of the worm trails that began to appear after the melting of the snow. Where I'm from, the full moon in September is most commonly called the Harvest Moon because that is when crops were traditionally gathered at the end of the summer season.

Write about what the full moons would be called if their names were based on the natural and cultural events in your own personal sphere. Perhaps "Bikini Moon," "Finals Moon," "Pumpkin Spice Moon," or "Mosquito Moon" can get you started.

March 14

On this day in 2025, my partner and I sur-*pi*-sed our friends and family when we announced we had eloped on Pi Day, so named because the infinitesimal number π or pi is often shortened to 3.14.

Since its beginnings at the San Francisco Exploratorium in the 1980s, Pi Day has become more of a cultural phenomenon, with people across the US observing the holiday annually by baking and eating a wide variety of pies whether sweet like apple or cherry or savory like chicken pot pie or pizza pie!

Today write about pie whether literally or figuratively. Maybe you feel inspired by your favorite flavor of pie, or maybe you want to write about a sweetie pie or someone being served humble pie.

March 15

Et tu, Brute? On this day in 44 BCE, Julius Caesar was assassinated by a throng of as many as 60 senators including his long-time friend, Brutus. Caesar's actual last words are unknown, though the phrase "Et tu, Brute?" (And you, Brutus?") was long-rumored and over a millennia later used in Shakespeare's play Julius Caesar through which the phrase grew widespread recognition as the ruler's supposed last words. It is used colloquially to demonstrate feelings of surprise betrayal, but some historians' interpretations suggest "Et tu, Brute" was a phrase and not a question. A common Roman proverb of the time stated, "And you too, my son, will have a taste of power," which more or less was used in the way we use "what goes around, comes around" today. So, if Caesar's last words were the equivalent of "What goes around, Brutus," the implication is that Caesar was warning Brutus of bad karma.

Write about a time you or someone you know succumbed to bad karma.

March 16

In her memoir *Heartbreak: A Personal and Scientific Journey*, author Florence Williams chronicles her quest to heal her broken heart using methods supported by science after she and her husband of twenty-five years divorced. Interestingly, as she writes in her book, some studies have shown that "rebounding," or becoming romantically involved soon after a breakup, actually improves health outcomes for the heartbroken even if that rebound relationship ends.

Today, break up with a piece of writing — even if only temporarily. Find a rebound project to throw all of your energy toward. Maybe it will be a whirlwind romance, maybe you will end up married to the idea. Maybe it will be a refreshing change, or maybe it will remind you of how much you love your original project.

March 17

March 17th is known across the globe as Saint Patrick's Day, a day to celebrate one's Irish heritage, wear green, attend parades and festivals, eat corned beef and cabbage, and drink Irish beer among other traditions.

Less commonly known, March 17th is also the feast day of Saint Gertrude, the patron saint of cats.

In today's writing, invoke the feline, whether it be an actual cat species, a character with catlike traits, a person named/nicknamed Cat, or other interpretation.

March 18

Pufferfish are naturally slow swimmers, making them a seemingly easy meal. However, when they detect a predator in pursuit, they fill their stretchy stomach with water until they appear spherical with the spines that cover their bodies pointed outward. If that's not enough to deter their predator, their bodies contain a neurotoxin that is lethal to most animals including humans.

Today, write about your own defense mechanisms.

March 19

The vernal equinox, the day on which we experience equal or near-equal amounts of daylight and darkness across all latitudes, marks the switch between winter and spring in the northern hemisphere. (In the southern hemisphere, they experience the autumnal equinox at this time.)

However, the vernal equinox is not necessarily the same day each year because our measure of time doesn't exactly line up with the Earth's orbit. So, the vernal equinox can occur anywhere between March 19th and 21st.

Write about daylight and darkness as if they were characters with human traits. What would they talk about? How would they interact? What conflicts would they have?

March 20

Fred Rogers was best known for hosting the popular children's series *Mister Rogers' Neighborhood* from 1968 to 2001. One of his most famous quotes first appeared in print in his 1983 book, *Mister Rogers Talks With Parents*: "When I was a boy and I would see scary things in the news, my mother would say to me, 'Look for the helpers. You will always find people who are helping.'"

Write about the people who helped you during a scary time. Write about when you helped someone who was experiencing something scary.

March 21

A long time ago I was a nanny for a little girl from the time she was two months old until she was two years old. As she was developing language, she used "babyisms" or sounds/words/phrases that represented actual words to her. For example, instead of saying "flower," she would say "yaya." Cauliflower? Cauli-yaya.

Include a dialogue with a young child and incorporate some unique babyisms in your writing today.

March 22

I live with a chronic illness called interstitial cystitis which causes painful symptoms similar to that of a urinary tract infection. One thing I had to give up entirely was caffeine as it was a huge contributor to the daily pain I experienced. Prior to my diagnosis, though, I was an extreme caffeine addict. My coffeemaker lived on my bedside table and acted as my alarm in the morning. I drank it black, so I would pour myself a cup before even getting out of bed. I drank coffee throughout the day and would sometimes even have a cup before going to sleep. I regularly drank caffeinated energy drinks and would sometimes pour coffee-flavored energy drinks into my regular coffee before drinking it. When I realized I had to give up coffee completely in order to mitigate my pain, I still had half a pot left from my daily brewing. I poured it down the drain while weeping. I have not had regular coffee or caffeine since.

Write about mourning the loss of an inanimate object.

March 23

On this day in 1775, at the second Revolutionary Convention in Virginia, Patrick Henry gave the speech at the end of which he famously declared, "Give me liberty or give me death!" while supposedly plunging a bone knife made of paper into his chest.

Write a speech on a topic important to you and conclude it with Henry's famous quote.

March 24

A "dead metaphor" is an expression that is so commonly used that even in brain scans, there's no indication that brains are deriving any additional meaning from them. For example, "He went on and on like a broken record" or "I fell head over heels in love." These are considered clichés, and writers want to avoid clichés like the plague! (wink)

Expanding on this concept, I propose the idea of "dead verbs," or verbs that are so often tied to certain nouns that their usage has become cliché and, therefore, less impactful. Some examples include, "tears streaming", "the sun shining", "a stomach growling", or "a heart breaking". Instead of "streaming" could tears "landslide"? Instead of "breaking" could a heart "splinter, one sliver at a time"?

Today, examine a piece of writing for dead verbs and replace any you find with fresh and unexpected images.

March 25

MASH is a children's game played to predict the future. The acronym stands for Mansion, Apartment, Shack, and House. (Though some variations list the S as street, sewer, shed, or swamp.) To start the game, MASH is written at the top of a piece of paper. In addition to housing, the game includes categories like potential career, spouse, what kind of car the player will drive, and more. After writing out the different possibilities, the fortuneteller draws a spiral on the page until the other person, who has their eyes closed, tells them to stop. The number of spirals drawn on the page becomes the number used to cross out the possibilities. Starting with the M in MASH, the fortuneteller points to each possibility while counting. Whichever possibility the number lands on is crossed out, and the game continues until only one possibility remains for each category, revealing the player's future.

Today, play a game of MASH. You can use the usual categories or create brand new ones. At the end of the game, use the result to inspire a piece of writing.

March 26

Dr. Daryl Davis is an R & B and blues musician as well as an anti-racist activist. He is well-known for befriending members from the racist hate group, the ku klux klan (KKK) and inspiring them to leave their white robes and hoods behind them. He claimed that the majority of the klansmen he met were victims of powerful brainwashing in their youth, and when they got to know him, a Black man, their prejudices eroded. After meeting and becoming friends with Davis, even the imperial wizard of the KKK in Maryland ended up leaving the klan and invited Davis to be his daughter's godfather.

Write about a time you questioned one or more of your beliefs. Who was the person and/or what were the circumstances that inspired your re-evaluation?

March 27

Ok, so maybe I'm stupid, but... one day when I was brushing my teeth at 38 years old, looking at the wide array of sprays and gels and goops on my bathroom sink, I realized I didn't know how sunscreen worked. So, I looked it up. If you are also a person who doesn't know, here's what I learned: Mineral sunscreens, which typically contain zinc or titanium, sit on the skin and act like a mirror to the sun. Ultraviolet rays are not able to penetrate the skin and cause sun damage because the minerals in the sunscreen reflect the rays away. Non-mineral sunscreens, on the other hand, contain chemicals like aminobenzoic acid, avobenzone, octisalate, octocrylene, and oxybenzone which absorb the ultraviolet radiation, preventing it from penetrating the skin and causing a sunburn.

Today, think about something that you take for granted but really don't understand how it works and write about it. Feel free to look up how the thing works and write about it accurately, or don't look it up and completely make it up!

March 28

The last confirmed sighting of an ivory-billed woodpecker happened in 1944. Since then the bird has been considered extinct or probably extinct by the American Birding Association, though it remains on the International Union for Conservation of Nature and Natural Resources' "critically endangered" list. The bird's primary habitat in woodland areas of Louisiana, Alabama, and Florida was destroyed by logging, and remaining birds were killed by hunters to add to their taxidermy collections. However, some ornithologists and avid bird watchers insist that they've seen ivory bills in the wild. The species has become a kind of Bigfoot or jackalope-esque urban legend.

Write from the perspective of the ivory-billed woodpecker or someone whose home/hometown/homeland was destroyed. Where might that individual relocate and/or go into hiding? What would they think of their new home?

March 29

In Celtic mythological traditions, bees were a kind of messenger between the human and more-than-human worlds. Beekeepers would tell their hives about significant happenings within the family so as to pass the messages along to their ancestors. Hives would often be decorated to commemorate marriages, births, and deaths.

Today, write what you would tell the bees in order for them to pass on the message to loved ones who have passed on. Bonus points for actually telling a bee about it if they're buzzing around in your neighborhood at this time of year.

March 30

In an interview with *The New York Times*, American singer-songwriter, Tracy Chapman, famous for her hits "Fast Car" and "Give Me One Reason" said, "I know that I have been labeled as a protest singer, and it's not a label that I accept. I'm not mad at it, but it doesn't fully represent what I do or how I think about myself."

Write about how you have been labeled. Who has labeled you? Are they labels you accept? Or do they not fully represent who you are or how you view yourself.

March 31

Mercury Stardust the "Trans Handy Ma'am" is an author, Trans activist, podcaster and TikToker famous for her educational videos on home repair. Her TikTok went viral after she posted a video explaining how to use a ratchet strap. Since then, her content has been viewed millions upon millions of times

In her book *Safe and Sound: A Renter-Friendly Guide to Home Repair* she writes, "We all come from different backgrounds with different lived experiences... But there is a universal truth: we all panic when the toilet overflows."

In today's writing, include the steps to repairing something. This could be literal like the steps to repairing a flat tire or snapped guitar string, or it could be metaphorical like how to fix a broken heart.

April 1

It's International Poetry Month and to celebrate, all of the prompts in April will be poetry-related.

Let's start with just the word "poem". It is derived from the Greek "poēma" meaning, literally, "a created thing."

Write about something you created that you feel really proud of. It can be a culinary dish, a joke, a work of art, a home, anything.

April 2

Hiram Sims is the co-founder and executive director of The Sims Library of Poetry located in Los Angeles, California. Before the library existed in brick and mortar, as a poetry teacher, Sims encouraged his students to read at least one poetry collection every week. Many of his students had a hard time acquiring different collections to read every week; they couldn't afford to buy new books, and the public library was sometimes too far or not easily reached through public transit. To meet his students' needs, he began carrying his own private collection of books to class in a suitcase. Friends and acquaintances began to donate their own poetry collections to the cause, and his suitcase expanded to his garage. Soon the garage could no longer hold the books either. His wife, Charisse, who was an early childhood educator, suggested they reimagine a nearby preschool into the Sims Library of Poetry, and so the dream was realized.

Write about what you would include if you had to fit a library into one suitcase. What significance do your choices hold? How did they shape who you are today?

April 3

My son was born on April 3rd after I had long-believed I wasn't destined to have children. As a poet, I was delighted to have given birth to him during National Poetry Month. I say he is "the best poem I'll ever write."

Write about a person or object or idea in your own life that is, in your opinion, the best non-poem poem that was ever written. What about it/them makes it/them poetry to you?

April 4

Eighteenth-century poet, Thomas Gray, is the person attributed to the common phrase "Ignorance is bliss." His exact wording from his poem "Ode on a Distant Prospect of Eton College" was "Where ignorance is bliss, 'tis folly to be wise."

With the communal knowledge of the world at our fingertips almost every moment of every day, write about the subjects, if any, you are willing to be ignorant about. What, if anything, are you willing to accept as "unknowable"?

April 5

One of the poetic trends filling up pages in literary magazines in recent years is Pulitzer Prize-winning poet Jericho Brown's invented poetic form the "duplex." The contemporary poetic form consists of 14 lines, arranged in couplets. The first line of the couplet repeats words/phrases verbatim or closely related to the previous line. For the last couplet, the last line repeats the very first line.

As Brown described in an article for The Poetry Foundation, a duplex is "a ghazal that is also a sonnet that is also a blues poem of 14 lines." He came up with the name "duplex" because "something about its repetition and its couplets made me feel like it was a house with two addresses."

Write a duplex (or not!) about the ways in which an aspect of your life is "a house with two addresses."

April 6

As of this writing, poet James Coats has invented at least three poetic forms including the 4 Kings, the mamba, and the *suplex*. The suplex is a play on Jericho Brown's duplex and a reference to a wrestling move that involves wrapping one's arms around their opponent, lifting the opponent off the ground, and then doing an extreme back bend that then flips and slams the opponent upside down into the mat behind.

Instead of creating sets of couplets in which the last line of one couplet becomes the first line of the next couplet like in the duplex, the suplex's first seven lines are flipped upside down to create this mirrored effect: Line (L)1 L2 / L3 L4/ L5 L6 / L7 L7 / L6 L5 / L4 L3 / L2 L1

In today's writing, maybe you'd like to attempt a suplex! If not, another way to *suplex* your writing might be to take something you have previously written and re-write it from the end to the beginning. Whether it be a poem or story, re-write it so the ending comes first and work your way back to the beginning.

April 7

Very few poets' poetry has made me laugh out loud, and only one has ever made me laugh out loud and then tear up in the same poem: Chen Chen.

In his poem "To the Guanacos at the Syracuse Zoo", the speaker recounts seeing Guanacos, a species closely related to the llama that is native to South America, for the first time.

"I'm sorry my boyfriend kept calling you / *guaca-moles* & I'm sorry I found that funny/" he wrote. "I'm sorry you were not llama-famous, & stuck / in an underfunded zoo in Upstate New York."

Okay, maybe you're not finding this funny. It's hard to capture the essence in just a quote. Go find the poem in the bonus materials and read it already!

In today's writing, attempt to begin with a joking or sarcastic tone, and then, see if you can find a poignant ending.

April 8

In his poem, "Synonyms for Maps," poet Arthur Kayzakian writes a kind of unnumbered list with each item separated with a vertical bar: "fence | an imaginary line... | an invention to value document over blood... | antithesis to holding hands... | a line denying strangeness from beauty | a strange boundary | can i please have some water | a phantom rule that promotes mortgage".

Taking a note from Kayzakian's poem, choose a subject to write synonyms for. Write them out in a list or include them in a poem. Maybe you want to expand upon the words in your list and explain why they're synonyms for this subject.

April 9

One of the most famous haiku was written sometime in the 17th century by Japanese poet and samurai Mizuta Masahide. It can be translated as, "My barn, having burned to the ground, I can now see the moon." He doesn't write that he is grateful his barn burned down. He isn't glad it happened. He simply notes his observation of now being able to see the moon.

Write about a time when you felt you lost everything. Dig deeply to find the metaphorical moon in that situation.

April 10

A hermit crab is a species of mollusk that scavenges for its outer shell as it grows. In poetry, a hermit crab is a poem placed into a non-poem container. That is to say, a poem that is written like an instruction manual, a recipe, a dictionary entry, a personal ad, an obituary, an electric bill, and so on.

Write a hermit crab. Choose a written document not usually associated with poetry. Study its format, how the text is arranged, and the tone. The subject can be related to the document or not! Write a recipe poem about going to a concert. Use the latest spam email in your inbox to structure a poem about your first kiss. The only rule is to find the most unexpected home for your poem.

April 11

In Martheaus Perkins' poem, "Hugging James Baldwin," the speaker has an imaginary experience interacting with the late, great poet. At the end, the speaker in the poem asks Baldwin for a hug. Perkins writes, "When he embraces me, / I'm caught by how wonderful it is to be fragile. / We're tugging at each other from both sides of history, / thread-backs tying together."

Imagine hugging a historical figure. What would the context for the embrace be? Who initiated? Is it awkward? Romantic? Playful? Or none of the above?

April 12

Poet, Noor ('Ditee) Jaber, invented a poetic form called the "colonial fit" in which a poem is written in English while employing Arabic grammatical rules. In an interview with the now defunct Vida Review she said "[The two languages] are incompatible, but they both belong in my mouth; I'm a Black person and an Arab; my mother's side of the family all speak English and my father's side speaks Arabic. The result of fitting the two languages into a single space is uncomfortable, and it should be."

If you speak another language, try writing in one language while using the grammatical rules of another. If you don't speak another language, try making up your own grammatical rules. For example, maybe all verbs appear before their subjects. So "The barking dog scared the crying baby" might turn into "Barking the dog scared crying the baby."

April 13

Renowned poet Sappho, who notably wrote romantic and erotic poetry for other women, lived on the Greek island of Lesbos which became the root of the word "lesbian." Although only a few hundred of her poetic lines remain—mostly in fragments—historians believe she likely produced over 10,000 in her lifetime. Many theories exist as to why her poetry was lost including one theory that suggests her work was destroyed by orders of Pope Gregory VII because of her reputation for promiscuity. Another theory claims her Aeolic dialect was difficult for readers to understand and therefore translate. And yet another theory postulates her poetry was lost when the library of Constantinople burned down in 1204.

To honor Sappho, write in admiration of a woman. Whether platonic, romantic, or erotic, let Sappho be your muse as you compose your tribute.

April 14

Cathy Park Hong's poem "Ballad in A" uses only the vowel "a" throughout the entire piece except for one instance of the vowel "i" in the word "I'll." (Though in some American dialects, the word "I'll" is pronounced with a twangy "a" sound, so I would argue that the use of the letter "i" was a play on word sounds, but I digress...)

Today, try to accomplish the same feat: write using exclusively (or almost exclusively) one vowel.

April 15

In her poetry collection *Hotel Almighty*, Sarah J. Sloat created erasure poems out of pages from Stephen King's novel *Misery*. However, she took the concept of erasure to a new level: Sloat created visual poetry out of her erasures using crayons, markers, collage, and even stitching.

Today, in homage to Sloat's work, let's create an artistic erasure. If you don't have art supplies, not to worry. You can let loose on the graphic art app of your choice. (Many apps like Canva have a free version.) Copy and paste a piece of writing into a blank document and create erasure through different colored font backgrounds, copy and pasting images from the internet, or whatever technique calls to you.

April 16

An abecedarian is a poem of 26 lines, each beginning with a letter of the alphabet A through Z in its traditional alphabetical sequence. Accomplishing the abecedarian is no easy feat, but if you'd like a warmup exercise before cannonballing into the form, you can start by simply creating a list of words in alphabetical order. They don't have to make any kind of sense or form any kind of coherent phrase, just list out the words. The next step would be to write a longer phrase for each letter. Again, the phrases don't have to make any sense when read together. Finally, the last step is to try your hand at the full thing where one line flows into the next.

Bonus: If you speak another language, you can attempt an abecedarian using that language's alphabet. For example, Franny Choi and Esther Kim have both written Hangul Abecedarians and the ʻōiwi Abecedarian can be found in Noʻu Revilla's collection *Ask the Brindled*.

April 17

Were you hoping for more fun with the abecedarian poetic form? Well I have good news for you!

Another style of abecedarian is called the phonetic abecedarian. Similar concept to the original, but in this case, the phonetic abecedarian focuses on the sound a word makes rather than the letter itself. For example, "apple" with it's short A sound wouldn't fit as an "a-word" in a phonetic abecedarian, but "able" or "Abraham Lincoln" would. The words "see" or "sea" could be used as the "c-word", but not the word "cat." Similarly, the word "excite" would work as an "x-word" but not the word "xylophone."

If you feel stuck, you can use the same warm-up exercises from yesterday to get the creative juices flowing.

April 18

A cento is a kind of poetic collage, borrowing each line from someone else's work. A cento can center one person's writing, borrowing lines from a single person's portfolio (using only Stevie Wonder lyrics, for example), or from an eclectic array of sources (for example, one line from a Mary Oliver poem, another line from grandma's apple kugel recipe, another from a set of Ikea directions, another from a Kendrick Lamar song, etc. etc.)

Create a piece of writing using only words borrowed from someone else.

April 19

A ribcage is not just the skeletal structure that houses the heart and lungs in the human body, it is also a poetic form! Invented by Athena Liu during The Speakeasy Project's Growth workshop led by torrin a. greathouse, a ribcage alternates twelve times between twelve-syllable lines and a monosyllabic word written in brackets. At the end of the poem, the bracketed words, or spine, are read from top to bottom.

Today, try your hand at a ribcage. (Pro Tip: Starting with the spine first, can be helpful!)

April 20

Concrete poetry also known as carmina figurate are poems that use words to physically create an image on the page. The words in my poem "Halfway", for example, are shaped like a hot-air balloon. The title poem from my chapbook *Mother, (v)* is shaped like a pregnant belly.

Whether you write a poem or not, endeavor to form the words on the page into the shape of something related to the writing itself.

April 21

In her poem, "Earth Day," Jane Yolen wrote, "I am the Earth / And the Earth is me. / Each blade of grass, / Each honey tree, / Each bit of mud, / And stick and stone / Is blood and muscle, / Skin and bone."

Write as if you were the Earth. What would you want to say to the populations? What would you want to tell yourself?

April 22

In his poem "Pollinator", poet Richard Davidson wrote, "I learned from the pollinators / that to touch / is existence".

Write about to what extent touch embodies or reaffirms one's existence.

April 23

An ode is a piece that glorifies a subject whether it be a person, place, event, or abstraction. Elizabeth Acevedo's "Rat Ode" lifts up a creature that normally gets a bad rap. Similarly Sharon Olds' "Ode to Dirt" shows appreciation for something people try to not get on themselves.

Write an ode for something that most people dislike but that you love.

April 24

As we saw from yesterday's prompt, an ode is a poem that glorifies a subject whether it be a person, place, event, or abstraction. An anti-ode is exactly what it sounds like: an opportunity to drag a subject through the mud.

What is it that you hate? Whether it's a heavy subject like genocide or white supremacy or something petty like someone saying "I'm going to share my screen now" before sharing their screen on Zoom, this is your opportunity to go off in an anti-ode.

April 25

In his collection *Deaf Republic*, Deaf poet Ilya Kaminsky wrote, "The deaf do not believe in silence. Silence is the invention of the hearing."

Write about a concept you might take for granted that you want to challenge as mere invention. Who invented it? Why? What purpose does this invention serve?

April 26

Personification occurs when human traits are attributed to an animal, inanimate object, or abstraction. For example, "The clouds smiled down on me." Clouds can't actually smile the way we know humans smile.

A persona poem is a poem in which the poet takes on the identity or point of view of someone other than themselves.

Putting the two together, a "Persona-fication Poem" is a poem in which the poet takes on the identity or point of view of an animal, inanimate object, or abstraction.

Let's try it out today!

April 27

American poet Douglas Kearney is known for what he calls "performative typography." His poems cross the boundaries into graphic design, and his performances of his poems are just as avant-garde. In an interview with the University of Minnesota, Kearney said "Working with visual poems started off for me as a way of turning the page into a stage space... the page is the stage, the stage is the page."

After researching Kearney's poems and performances (you can find examples in this book's bonus content using the QR code at the beginning of the book), use them as inspiration for how your writing (whether it's something you've already written or have yet to write) appears on the page.

April 28

In her powerful poem "we hold these truths to be self-evident" that she performed for the "Writers for Migrants" event in 2019, bridgette bianca uses the famous phrase from the American Declaration of Independence as an anaphora, or a kind of repeated refrain that anchors the stanzas in her piece as she calls out hypocrisies and calls for a deepening sense of humanity.

In today's writing, explore the use of anaphora. Is there a phrase, whether famous or not, that can appear at the beginning of each stanza? If not writing a poem, aim to repeat the phrase three or more times in your piece.

April 29

Attributed to Sei Shonagon as demonstrated in her collection *The Pillow Book*, the zuihitsu—Japanese for "following the brush"—is a style of poem that weaves together bits and pieces of the author's thoughts—some prose, some lineated poetry, some lists, any style of writing —as a kind of collage of a moment in time.

In 2006, Kimiko Hahn's collection, *The Narrow Road to the Interior*, brought the zuihitsu into a modern light. Hahn describes the zuihitsu as "rooms created by the little blocks of text."

Write a zuihitsu. Follow your pen wherever it wants to take you. What does each little "room" contain?

April 30

On April 30, 2023, my first poetry collection, *Survived By: A Memoir in Verse + Other Poems*, debuted. On the back cover I wrote "These lines helped me survive. Do what you need with them to survive too. Draw on these pages. Or tear them out. Carry a poem in your pocket. Or give it to someone else. Cross out my words and write your own. Make a collage. Use them as kindling. Just show me what you create."

Today, take someone else's writing and recreate it so that it is more meaningful to you by writing over the writer's words with your own.

May 1

As of 2025, seaweed farming is the fastest growing aquaculture sector in the world. In recent years, aquatic farmers across the globe have switched from farming fish and other aquatic animals to farming seaweed because it grows so fast, it doesn't need fertilizers or pesticides, it doesn't need any fresh water to grow, and it can help clean polluted water! Seaweed is found in lots of everyday products including toothpaste and makeup, but is also often found in many food products like sauces, salsas, and candy!

Write from the perspective of a farmer. What is a major crop where you live? What aspects of local weather, landscape, and/or politics might influence a farmer's business?

May 2

Verbal dyspraxia is a condition caused by brain signals not communicating with the muscles responsible for speech. Someone with verbal dyspraxia can understand language but aren't able to produce it themselves. Many people living with verbal dyspraxia rely on speech-producing devices to speak on their behalf. One man from the United Kingdom had a custom voice created for him that combined the voices of two other British men together so that his proxy voice no longer sounded like a mechanical robot. When he first received the new voice, his mother asked him to say "I love you, mum" over and over and over again.

Make a list of voices that are important to you. If you could only hear each voice say one unique phrase, what would you want to hear each voice say?

May 3

Did you have an imaginary friend as a child? My imaginary friends were the characters from Gotham City: Batman, Robin, Catwoman, The Joker, and the like. Usually in my scenarios, I was the mediator who settled their conflicts!

Write about an imaginary friend, whatever that may mean to you.

May 4

Matty Benedetto is a product designer who has created and trademarked over 350 products that are intentionally useless. On his website, for example, he has a pair of "Sloppy Slacks;" jeans that have towels sewn into the tops of the thighs for wiping hands when eating gets messy.

Write something with the intention of it being a wacky piece of writing with no real purpose other than to delight.

May 5

Have you ever experienced "The Ick"? It's a feeling of disgust derived from something someone you date does that negatively alters the way you feel about them. The Ick is different from a red flag. Whereas red flags are rather serious warnings about a person's character or behavioral patterns, The Ick is caused by something innocuous. For example, I went to dinner with a very nice guy. He even brought me flowers for our date. But when our meals came, he unironically tucked his napkin into his shirt. We never had a second date. Another time, I had been on a few dates with a woman, and I really liked her! But she kept giving me gifts. The first was a little vase of flowers. Okay, that's cute. Then it was a pair of earrings. Next it was a hat. Then one day she came over with a set of stereo speakers that she wanted to give me despite me not having a television or stereo or anything to use the speakers with. It was too much! Was she trying to buy my affections? I immediately got The Ick.

Write about your experience with The Ick.

May 6

The constellation Ursa Major, also known as the Big Dipper or the Great Bear, appears in the northern hemisphere beginning in the spring. According to Greek mythology, Zeus transformed the beautiful Callisto into a bear to protect her from jealous Hera. Mythology from Southwestern Asia instead describes the Big Dipper as a coffin with the stars in the constellation's "handle" acting as mourners following behind. In Northern European traditions, the Big Dipper represents a wagon. In Ancient England it was referred to as King Arthur's chariot, and to the Inuit people, the star pattern represents a caribou.

Today write your own constellation story either for the Big Dipper or for a constellation of your choice.

May 7

As weird as this sounds, I sleep with a pillow *over* my head. In fact, I have a hard time falling asleep if I don't have a pillow on my head. I don't remember how this started, if my household was particularly noisy as a child and so I slept with a pillow over my head to drown out the din, or some other origin story. Somehow this came up at one of my book clubs, and one of my book club friends revealed that she sleeps completely face down, not just on her belly, but with her face planted into the mattress.

In today's writing, incorporate someone's unusual sleep habits.

May 8

In observance of Mother's Day that takes place in the US around this time of year, the next two prompts reference my poetry collection *Mother, (v)* [pronounced "Mother comma verb"]. I wrote this collection as I was entering my late thirties and was filled with anxiety about my window of opportunity to become a parent narrowing. About the collection, one reviewer wrote it was "pregnant with longing and a desire to love" that it was "both a meditation on and plea for motherhood."

Write about something you are pleading for.

May 9

In the title poem of my collection *Mother, (v)*, I described my non-parenthood as a list of all the things I did or did not do, all the things I could or could not do because of my non-parenthood. "[N]o handprints on mirrors no play-doh crusted into carpet... no pint-sized toothbrush leans against mine no toys in primary colors line the tub's edge... my lips have never kissed a bruise... i go by no other name..."

Write a description of yourself, another person, or an object as a list of things that are missing from your (or their or its) everyday life.

May 10

Many people throughout history have changed their names as a symbol of rebirth. Acclaimed author Toni Morrison went by the name Chloe until she was baptized in the Catholic faith at age twelve at which time she took on the baptismal name Anthony, which led to her nickname, Toni. Famed boxer Muhammad Ali, né Cassius Clay, took on his new name after converting to Islam. Though he later reverted to his original stage name, rapper Snoop Dogg changed his name to Snoop Lion after converting to Rastafarianism.

Whether for religious reasons or not, write about what name you might go by if not by your current name. Have you thought about using a pen name or changing your name all together? How come? What might your hypothetical new name symbolize in your life?

May 11

Richard Feynman earned the Nobel Prize in Physics in 1965 and famously coined the question, "If, in some cataclysm, all of scientific knowledge were to be destroyed, and only one sentence was passed on to the next generation of creatures, what statement would contain the most information in the fewest words?" His response was "I believe it is the atomic hypothesis that all things are made of atoms—little particles that move around in perpetual motion, attracting each other when they are a little distance apart, but repelling upon being squeezed into one another. In that one sentence, you will see, there is an enormous amount of information about the world, if just a little imagination and thinking are applied."

Write what you would want to pass on to the next generation of creatures if you had to contain the most information in the fewest words.

May 12

The platypus is a most-fascinating creature. Not only is it one of only four mammal species that lay eggs, it is also one of the only few mammals that are *venomous*. Male platypuses have a spur on their foot that can deliver painful venom. Their famous bill contains tens of thousands of electroreceptors which allows them to use electrolocation to find prey in murky water.

Write a literary platypus. If a platypus has a bill like a duck, a tail like a beaver, feet like an otter, electroreceptors like a shark, venom like a scorpion, and eggs like a reptile, maybe a literary platypus derives its elements from a variety of sources. A poem with the title at the end à la Rupi Kaur, with the humor of Brian Bilston, the structure of a sonnet, the language of Ocean Vuong, and so on.

May 13

When was the last time you played in the dirt? Research published in the *The Journal of Allergy and Clinical Immunology* suggests exposure to and playing in the dirt as a kid can lead to better health outcomes throughout life like a reduced likelihood of developing allergies or asthma. But playing in the dirt can be good for your health as an adult too! Some findings published in the journal *Neuroscience* suggest that certain bacteria living in soil can stimulate the release of serotonin, working similarly to an antidepressant.

Ready to play in the dirt? Before writing today, get your hands in some soil. Watch as it crumbles between your fingers. Rub it against your fingertips. Maybe give it a big whiff. Taste it? No, you don't have to go that far. Just get a little... dirty. Include the sensory experience in your writing today.

May 14

When I was in preschool, my sister taught me a song that she learned when she was in preschool called "Magic Penny". This song, written by Malvina Reynolds compares love to a "magic penny," saying that if you try to keep it just to yourself, you'll end up with none, but if you are generous with it, you'll end up with an abundance.

Write about to what extent this paradox holds true for you.

May 15

In Korean, "keum-boo" translates to "attached gold" and refers to an ancient jewelry-making technique in which gold foil and silver are fused together. During the heating and pressing processes, the gold and silver atoms meld together creating beautiful, high-contrast designs.

Write about two beautiful people, places, or things melding together to form an even greater beauty.

May 16

Historically, a doppelgänger was considered to be an evil ghostly twin of a living person. Today, the term is used more so to describe someone who looks just like someone else despite not being related. My doppelgänger even has a similar name as mine: Anna May. We look so much alike that at a concert, a stranger came up to me and punched me in my arm. When I turned around scowling, the person apologized, explaining they thought I was Anna May, and they were coming to say hi. Another time, a stranger added me as a friend on Facebook, and when I asked if we knew each other, she said, "Yeah! I was the hitchhiker you picked up on the way to the ski resort yesterday!" I texted Anna May asking, "Did you pick up a hitchhiker on your way to the ski resort yesterday?" and sure enough...

Write about your doppelgänger. Even if you don't have one that you know of, make it up!

May 17

Besides having a doppelgänger who looks very much like me, I also have a name twin: *another* Anne Marie Wells. And get this, she is also an author! (Though her niche is Christian graphic novels.) She and I have never met, but I see her everywhere on the internet and on book listing sites. Then there is an *Annie* Wells (my nickname, and the name I mostly went by as a child) who is a Pulitzer Prize-winning photographer! And one time when I searched my name on the internet in college, I found another Anne Marie Wells who was a reiki healer. She and I even had an eerily similar appearance, and one of our photos was taken in the exact same pose! I don't know what happened to that Anne Marie Wells. Internet searches to reconnect haven't been fruitful. Anyway, shout out to all the *other* Anne Marie / Annie / Anne Wellses out there.

Do an internet search of your name, and write a story about this other person. If you have a particularly unique name, try searching for just your first or last name instead.

May 18

Though they are mostly associated with the Netherlands and Dutch culture, tulip festivals take place all across the globe. The largest tulip festival, however, takes place in Ottawa, Ontario, Canada every year.

During WWII, the Canadian military led the efforts that liberated the Netherlands from Nazi occupation, and Canada became the refuge for the Dutch royal family who fled after Germany invaded.

As a tribute to this special history, every year the Dutch royal family, as well as other Dutch entities, send tulip bulbs to Ottawa's tulip festival.

Write about a person with whom you have a special relationship thanks to an act of kindness.

May 19

Laila Ali, daughter of famous boxer Muhammad Ali, retired from her own professional boxing career undefeated. She held multiple titles both nationally and internationally, and is considered not just one of the best *female* boxers of all-time, but one of the best *boxers* of all-time. Period.

Write about the ways in which you hope your children (either real or hypothetical) take after you. Write about the ways you hope they surpass you.

May 20

Slime molds are one of the most misunderstood forms of life on the planet. They are not a fungi, plant, or animal. They actually exist in their own kingdom called Protista. Studies have shown that despite not having a brain, slime molds travel and can even navigate mazes. They find the most efficient routes to food sources and leave slime trails behind them so they can "remember" where they have already been. Even though many people find them to be icky, they are essential to healthy ecosystems, acting as decomposers breaking down decaying detritus.

Many people confuse slime molds with fungi, but surprisingly, humans are actually more closely related to fungi than slime molds are! Compared to slime molds, fungi might as well be our cousins!

Write about your relationship with a cousin or distant relative.

May 21

In the English language, the word "set" has the most definitions of any other word. It can act as a verb: to set an object down, beside, or atop another object. It can act as a noun: a train set, a chess set, a set of clothes. It can act as an adjective: I'm all set! Then, there are a whole slew of meanings when different modifiers are attached to it: set up, set down, set in, set out, set off, set on, set about, set back. Geesh!

In today's writing, try to use the word set in as many different ways as you can.

May 22

Many social studies have affirmed that expressing gratitude improves not only mental health metrics but physical health metrics, too. I don't disagree with these studies at all, but for me, keeping a gratitude journal or recounting what I am grateful for can lead to a sense of guilt, that I am not grateful enough for a roof over my head or the food that I ate. Sometimes, the recounting can feel kind of trite, like I'm just going through the motions: "Yes, I'm grateful for the roof over my head, again today. Yes, I'm grateful for the food I ate, again today."

Instead, every night before bed, my husband and I recount the different instances that *delighted* us. It's a nice inventory of the things that went well or the cute things that our son said or did. For example, I saw cute ducklings crossing the street with their mom. I'm not *grateful* I saw cute ducklings, but it did *delight* me.

Write about what delighted you today or recently.

May 23

Founder of Mama's Kitchen Press, Camari Carter Hawkins, once suggested to her followers that if you are struggling to meet goals or make dreams come true, it helps to collaborate with others because you're less likely to let others down than you are to let yourself down.

Write about a time you collaborated with someone else. Was it a positive or negative experience? Bonus points if you collaborate with someone else on this writing!

May 24

Simone Biles is considered the greatest gymnast of all time. She not only earned eleven Olympic medals and thirty World Championship medals, making her the most decorated gymnast of all time, but she also has five gymnastics moves named after her for having been the first person to successfully complete each of them at an international competition.

And believe it or not, it all started at age six when she went on a daycare field trip to a gymnastics facility.

Write about a trip or experience you had as a child that influenced your formative years.

May 25

Nineteenth-century, American philosopher, essayist, minister, lecturer, abolitionist, and poet Ralph Waldo Emerson is attributed with the quote, "I cannot remember the books I've read any more than the meals I have eaten; even so, they have made me."

In today's writing, include an unforgettable book and an unforgettable meal.

May 26

Alexis Nikole Nelson aka the Black Forager, has garnered millions of followers across her social media channels by showing people the delicious and nutritious foods that are growing right in front of them; no Instacart fee necessary!

In an interview with Atmos she said, "If there's one thing I want people to walk away from my content with, it's thinking more deeply about any of the food they're consuming, whether they grew it, found it themselves or picked it up at the grocery store. I just want folks to be a bit more curious, open-minded and whimsical about the food that they're choosing to consume."

Write about where your food came from down to the ingredients. Where does it come from? Who harvested the wheat or coffee fruits or peanuts? How did those ingredients make their way into the food you ate? How did they make their way to the place you purchased them? You don't have to do the research if you don't want to. You can just use your imagination.

May 27

In her comedy special "Father", Atsuko Okatsuka joked, "I was a cheerleader in high school, so I'm very 'yes and' energy." She continued saying cheerleading is "blindly pumping people up to think they're gonna win even if you have no say in the game... [it's] the only sport where you're supporting another sport that people are actually there to see."

I feel this deeply since I, too, was a cheerleader in high school. Not only was I the cheer captain in 2003, but I had been cheering since I was eight years old. I feel my most confident when I am cheering others on, encouraging them to go big, and letting them know I'm still proud of them even if they fall short. But, on the flip side, I struggle to provide the same encouragement to myself.

In today's writing, cheer for yourself. Encourage yourself, congratulate yourself, root for yourself. Go! Go! Go!

May 28

In one of her works from her Arbol de la Vida or Tree of Life series, artist Ana Mendieta photographed herself with her arms raised and caked head to toe (including her hair) with mud standing at the base of a tree. The effect makes her appear as if she is part of the tree itself or even being birthed as if by mitosis from the tree. The line between where the tree ends and she begins becomes blurred.

In today's writing, camouflage yourself somehow in your words so the line between where you end and your writing begins becomes blurred.

May 29

In 2010, Itaru Sasaki, a Japanese garden designer, built an old-fashioned phone booth and installed a rotary telephone. Inside, there were no wires connecting it to any electrical outlets or phone jacks. Instead, he used the phone booth to "call" his cousin who had passed away from cancer. In an interview with a Japanese broadcasting network, he said, "Because my thoughts couldn't be relayed over a regular phone line, I wanted them to be carried on the wind." He called the installation Kaze No Denwa, "The Wind Phone."

Whether you knew them personally or not, imagine calling an ancestor on The Wind Phone. Write out your conversation.

May 30

When I was earning my certificate in social emotional arts through the Arts & Healing Initiative, one project I was assigned was to interview someone much younger than I was about their favorite music—musicians, bands, and/or songs. The exercise made me contemplate the music that was important to me as a teenager and how when I tried to share my love of The Get Up Kids, Taking Back Sunday and other emo bands of the era with my parents, they... didn't get it. Hahaha!

Today, ask a person much younger than you about their favorite music and what they like about it. Make note and then, if you are able, find a sample to play in the background while you write. Imagine a scenario in which either the person you interviewed or someone else might be listening to this song, band, or genre of music.

May 31

Eric Moussambani gained international notoriety as a swimmer after he represented Equatorial Guinea in the 2000 Olympic Games despite having only trained for eight months before his race. The Olympics offered wild card entries to countries with emerging economies that lacked training facilities. When he was the only person to show up for the call, he became Equatorial Guinea's Olympian. He had never even seen an Olympic-size swimming pool before arriving in Sydney; he had trained in lakes and a hotel swimming pool where management allowed him access for one hour a day between 5 and 6 AM. The two other competitors in the heat were disqualified for false starting, making Moussambani the automatic winner to move forward to the final. He became the first person to have qualified for the final with a time slower than all of recorded Olympic history. As he struggled to reach the finish line, the crowd of 17,000 spectators erupted cheering for him.

Write about shooting your shot despite the odds being against you.

June 1

Pearl is the birthstone for those born in June. Pearls can only be formed by oysters and mussels if an irritant has snuck in between their shells. The creature will cover the irritant in nacre, the material that forms the inside of the shells. Its smoothness prevents the irritant from harming the animal and creates what humans find to be precious. The infamous black pearl is created by the black-lipped *Pinctada margaritifera* species of oyster which creates a black nacre.

Write about an irritant in your life that could benefit from being covered in a metaphorical nacre. How can something harmful be made innocuous, even if only hypothetically?

June 2

Nacho Garrido is an illustrator and animator whose credits include Disney Channel, PBS Kids, Nickelodeon, Sesame Street, and many many video games. Though he is a modern animator living in Okinawa, Japan, a country known for its technological innovations, he has an affinity for vintage or "retro" games and video games, particularly hand-held gaming devices that predate Nintendo's Game Boy.

Imagine the machines or techniques that would be employed to do your job in the past and write about it. For example, if you're a writer who uses laptop computers and online software to create your works, what would it be like to have to buy sheets of paper and write using a quill and ink? If you have a more modern profession like social media marketing, imagine what it would be like having to market a product before computers, before regulated postal services, or before the printing press.

June 3

Étienne Bottineau was a lesser member of the French naval engineering corp in the 18th century. Before the invention of radar to detect the positioning of enemy ships, Bottineau developed the art of "nauscopie" or being able to detect sailing ships at a great distance, even hundreds upon hundreds of miles beyond the horizon, farther than even telescopes could see. His ability to reliably predict the arrival of sailing ships led those in positions of power to accuse him of sorcery! But instead of witchcraft, Bottineau said he spent countless hours studying the horizon until he understood the predictable changes in the atmosphere, wind, and sea or "emanations" produced by a boat.

If you could predict the entrance of someone or something, what would you want to be able to predict? Write about how and what you would need to study in order to hone your craft.

June 4

Mockingbirds are known for their uncanny ability to mimic sounds. It's not just other birds' songs that they mimic, they can sound like trilling toads, chirping crickets, meowing cats, barking dogs, and even squeaking doors. A male mockingbird (who sings more than a female mockingbird) can learn around 200 songs throughout his lifetime and sing a different repertoire of songs depending on the season.

Write about a song that is special to your life story.

June 5

Dr. Julia McDonald is a poet and OB/GYN. Her poetry collection *Hysteriography* was "birthed from intimate conversations" about uteruses, menstruation, pregnancy, abortion, loss, and childbirth.

While in a poetry workshop led by her, she asked the group to write either the story of our first period, or our first experience learning about periods. Though we didn't go around the circle sharing what we wrote, just being asked to reflect on my own experience made me realize just how much of a taboo subject periods still are.

Today, I invite you to do the same exercise: write either about your first period, or if you have never had a period, write about your experience learning about periods. Were there any myths or misconceptions you believed? How did you unlearn the misinformation?

June 6

Bisa Butler is an incredible textile artist. By layering scraps of neon-colored and traditional African fabrics, she creates breathtaking, life-sized, quilted portraits, many of which portray individuals and scenes from Black American history. Her textile art has been featured on magazine covers, exhibited all over the world, and earned her many awards.

In a feature for DearBlackWomenProject.com, she is quoted as saying, "I have always been drawn to portraits. I was the little girl who would sit next to my grandmother and ask her to go through her old family photo albums. I was the one who wanted to hear the story behind every picture."

Using an old family photo as inspiration, create a literary portrait of the person or people in the picture.

June 7

To celebrate the installation of Iván Argote's seventeen-foot tall pigeon sculpture titled "Dinosaur" at the Spur on the High Line, a public park in New York City, the caretaking group, Friends of the High Line, organized Pigeon Fest which, among its many offerings, featured the first-ever Pigeon Impersonation Pageant.

Participants donned pigeon-inspired costumes, strutted, pecked, had bread crumbs thrown at them, and did their best cooing to woo a panel of judges. The winner was Miriam Abrahams who spent weeks crafting her costume from chicken wire and papier-mâché.

Today, write from the perspective of a pigeon, whether it be traditionally sized, human-sized, or seventeen feet tall.

June 8

Narwhals are the unicorns of the sea, with a spiraled tusk jutting from their head which can grow up to ten feet long! Contrary to popular belief, narwhals don't use their tusks for either hunting or self-defense. Generally, only males grow tusks, and even then, some males' tusks never grow! So what would be the purpose for this giant appendage? Some researchers believe the tusk may help the animals detect shifts in water temperature, pressure, and salinity. Additionally, it might act as an indicator of sexual fitness. In other words, male narwhals with substantial tusks might be considered more appealing to female narwhals who want only the best genetics for their offspring.

Write about the characteristics you find most appealing when looking for a companion.

June 9

A practice I find somewhat challenging is loving-kindness meditation. There are, of course, many methods of practice, but the method I have learned begins with visualizing someone close to you like a child, spouse, or best friend. Then you send loving-kindness to them through your mind, heart, and spirit, praying (or wishing) they be happy, healthy, and free of harm. Then you repeat the exercise while thinking about an acquaintance; someone you know, but not well. Then you repeat the exercise while thinking about a familiar stranger; a person you recognize from the grocery store, for example, but whose name you don't know. Then you repeat the exercise while thinking of someone who is annoying to you; a rude coworker or obnoxious in-law. Lastly, you repeat the exercise while thinking of someone you hate; someone you wish bad karma upon. And yes, then you wish them to be happy, healthy, and free of harm too.

Why not try it today? Write out a list of people who meet these different criteria and your well wishes for them.

June 10

Before European colonizers took over the region known today as California, the area is believed to have had the greatest diversity of Indigenous languages in North America. Many tribal communities were isolated due to California's unique geography, which contributed to the linguistic distinctions. The California Language Archive (CLA) estimates between 80 and 90 different languages were spoken by over 500 communities.

According to the CLA website, "[I]t is not possible to distinguish scientifically between a 'language' and a 'dialect,'" noting that "political or social distinctions often play a role."

While considering regional, generational, cultural and/or other influences, what words or phrases are unique to your dialect? Use these terms and expressions in your writing today.

June 11

Clinical psychologist, Dr. Becky Kennedy, believes that boredom is "the feeling all of us have before [we experience] creativity, independence, and flexibility." Sandi Mann, author of *The Science of Boredom* and Jonathan Smallwood who teaches cognitive neuroscience at Queen's University in Kingston, Ontario would probably agree with this sentiment. Smallwood claims that smartphones have eliminated boredom from our modern lives because we can "play games, phone people, [and] we can check the internet." Mann's research has shown that minds *need* to wander and be idle in order for them to have the self-reflection time that begets creativity. "You come up with really great stuff when you don't have that easy lazy junk food diet of the phone to scroll all the time," she said.

Today, try to be bored all day. If you can't be bored all day, try one hour. If you can't be bored for an hour, try fifteen minutes. Literally just sit or lie down and do nothing except think. When you get up, do some writing, and see what happens.

June 12

In the United States, June 12th is Loving Day, which commemorates the 1967 Supreme Court decision in the Loving v. Virginia case that abolished state laws that prevented interracial couples from marrying.

Let's celebrate Loving Day with some loving. Write about a couple whose love you admire, whether real or fictitious.

June 13

FOMO, the Fear Of Missing Out, became a regular part of English-speaking vernacular in the early 2000s and 2010s. The acronym was used to express a negative feeling associated with being absent from potentially fun or fulfilling activities.

Pushing back against the "FOMO" phenomenon, blogger Aril Dash is attributed with coining the term "JOMO," or the *Joy* Of Missing Out, a feeling of relief or glee associated with not being at a certain event or partaking in a certain activity, even if it appears others are really enjoying themselves.

Write about an event or activity you're happy to miss out on. For example, I know that skydiving is on many people's list of things they want to experience before they die. I am not one of those people. Even if I learned every single one of my friends were going to go skydiving together, I'd say, "Y'all have fun. I'm staying home."

June 14

Malala Yousafzai is the youngest person, as of this writing, to have received the Nobel Peace Prize. She became internationally known after she survived an attempted assassination by the Taliban because of her unrelenting activism in Pakistan, fighting for the right for girls to attend school. Despite the threats to her life, she became even more steadfast in her activism, co-founding the Malala Fund and co-authoring the best-selling book *I Am Malala*.

While at the ceremony in Norway where she accepted her Nobel Prize, a Mexican college student interrupted the ceremony to protest the abduction of 43 male students from Iguala, Guerrero, Mexico. Instead of being annoyed, Yousafzai supported him saying, "[I]t is really important that children raise their voices."

Write about a time you raised (or wished you raised) your voice as a child or young adult.

June 15

The Latin phrases "HIC SVNT DRACONES" and "HIC SVNT LEONES" were commonly used by cartographers during the Middle Ages to denote the parts of maps that were considered unknown or uncharted. The phrases translate to "Here be dragons" and "Here be lions," respectively. Often, cryptid beasts would be drawn in those spots to indicate the potential dangers that lie within.

Whether in the physical or abstract realms, write about the areas in the world or in your life you would label with "HIC SVNT DRACONES". Are you a city person who would be terrified to travel alone in a dense forest? Or are you a person from a more rural area who feels stressed when driving the busy highways of metropolises? Or maybe you come from a warm climate and so exploring the North Pole would be a hard no for you. Maybe you would label the idea of becoming a parent or living without modern technology with "HIC SVNT DRACONES". Whatever it is, now is the time to explore where the dragons and lions be.

June 16

Embodied healing coach, Syanna Wand, once wrote, "How to hold regret tenderly: I wish I would have done that differently, and, at the time, I couldn't."

Write about something you regret. Can you hold it tenderly now? What do you wish you could have done differently but at the time wasn't able to?

June 17

Certain species of cicada spend 17 years of their lives underground as nymphs, their juvenile form. When they've reached maturity and are ready to reproduce, millions of cicadas will emerge at the same time in what's called a "mass emergence." Similarly, some species of flowers will lie dormant for years, particularly in desert regions. Then after an extraordinarily wet rainy season, these flowers will blossom all at the same time in what's called a "superbloom".

Imagine your own metaphorical "mass emergence" or "superbloom". Write about you and all of your loved ones reaching pinnacles in your lives and experiencing massive success all at the same time. Even if you don't feel like it has happened (yet!), use your imagination. If you feel called, you can use today's writing as a kind of prayer or manifestation.

June 18

Have you ever seen someone magnet fishing before? Crime scene investigators sometimes use giant magnets to find discarded weapons in bodies of water, but some people use them for treasure hunting since the giant magnet will attract anything metallic. Sure, they might pull up a tire rim or beer can, but one couple hooked a safe in New York with contents worth around $100,000! Whether trash or treasure is found, magnet fishing is a fun activity that also helps clean up aquatic environments. It's a win-win!

Write about a win-win situation.

June 19

After the end of the American Civil War, years passed before all enslaved people were finally free due to the fact that former confederate states weren't heeding the Emancipation Proclamation signed by President Lincoln. In response to confederate states' refusal, Mr. Lincoln sent Union troops into southern states to enforce the new federal law. It wasn't until June 19, 1865 when enslaved people were finally freed in Texas that the legal trafficking and enslavement of human beings was definitively abolished in The United States (except when subjected to the American carceral system).

Write about the unequivocal end of something whether it be the enslavement of human beings in the United States or other subject.

June 20

The summer solstice (which can take place either June 20th, 21st, or 22nd) attracts tourists from all over the world to Stonehenge. Every June people gather at the henge in England to witness the sunrise align with the henge's Heel Stone and shine into the center of the monument.

In honor of the summer solstice, write about an event that happened at the exact perfect time.

June 21

A portmanteau is the combination of two words to create a new word. It's different from compound words like "snowman" or "tailgate" in which the two words are easily distinguishable. Instead, a portmanteau is really a blending of two words. For example, Juneteenth from a couple days ago is a portmanteau of June and nineteenth. One of the most common portmanteaux is "brunch" which combines the words breakfast and lunch.

Today, invent your own portmanteau and use it in your writing. My invention (as far as I know) is "suppert" or when you eat dessert for supper (like whenever I go out to eat at The Cheesecake Factory and order their red velvet cheesecake with the white chocolate ganache as my meal, I'm having suppert. *drool*)

June 22

Wangechi Mutu is a Kenyan-American multi-media artist who creates collage art as well as sculpture, film, and performance art. Many of her pieces have mythological or whimsical elements such as her sculpture MamaRay which depicts a kind of supernatural creature with a human-like head and a manta ray body.

In a feature on ThisIsAfrica.me, she is quoted as saying "Art allows you to imbue the truth with a sort of magic."

Today write a true story, but imbue it with some magical elements.

June 23

Before the Aswan High Dam was constructed in 1970 to control water flow, generate hydroelectric energy, and enable regulated irrigation, the Nile river would flood every year. This flooding was essential to not just Egyptian life, but to the many farming communities along the river's 4,000+ mile (6,000 km) span. When the river's levels returned to normal, deposits of black silt that were rich in vitamins and minerals were left behind, which allowed crops to thrive in the desert. Without it, many if not all of the civilizations would have perished.

Today, take a piece of writing and flood it with imagery. Make sure each noun is drenched in description. Even if this version of the piece is not the final iteration, perhaps there will be metaphorical deposits of nutrient-dense silt left after the next revision.

June 24

In her essay "Cicada Magic" published in *Orion Magazine*, Nikole Brown writes, "Go ahead, call them an *invasion*. Use that word of war... but know you're using it for an insect... who spreads no disease, eats no crops, chews no holes..."

I have to admit, after reading her essay, I had a change of heart for the ugly things.

She goes on to write, "Better yet, call them a *benevolence*, peaceful as they are, doing little harm, aerating the soil with their many tunnels as they dig their way up and out, then fertilizing that soil when their bodies surrender to that same ground."

In today's writing, create your own version of "Cicada Magic" or replace "Cicada" with another creature you have previously considered... kinda gross. What kind of magic does this creature have to offer?

June 25

Eric Carle was one of the most famous children's book illustrators, having famously written and illustrated *The Very Hungry Caterpillar* among many other works in his bibliography. His iconic story centers on a caterpillar who, in the days leading up to building a cocoon, fills his belly with a number of different foods, eating more and more as the week progresses. On Saturday, the story recounts the caterpillar ate through a long list of foods including chocolate cake, an ice cream cone, a pickle, a slice of Swiss cheese, a slice of salami, a lollipop, a piece of cherry pie, a sausage link, a cupcake, and a slice of watermelon.

Include a long list of food items in your writing today.

June 26

Margaret Keane was a painter best known for creating whimsical people and animals with enormous eyes. Initially her husband at the time, Walter Keane, claimed credit for her paintings, going as far as exhibiting them across the country under his own name. After they divorced, Margaret came forward as the true artist and sued her ex-husband for claiming credit. During the trial, the judge ordered Margaret and Walter to both create one of the iconic paintings. Walter claimed he had a shoulder injury and couldn't participate. Then Margaret finished her painting in less than an hour. She was awarded $4 million in damages, but the award was overturned in appeals court. Despite never seeing a penny, Margaret said she didn't care about the money, but only wanted to be credited as the true artist.

Write about reclaiming something that is rightfully yours.

June 27

Helen Keller was an American author, lecturer, and activist famous for having been the first Deafblind American to earn a bachelor's degree. She attributes her success to her compassionate teacher Anne Sullivan who taught Keller how to use sign language in the palm of her hand and later to read lips by touching them with her fingers. The anecdote of Sullivan placing Keller's hands under water from a well pump and then signing "water" into her palm over and over until Keller made the connection between the two has been famously depicted in both the stage play and film *The Miracle Worker*, which are adaptations of Keller's memoir *The Story of My Life*.

Though Keller died more than three decades after Sullivan, Keller's ashes were interred at the National Cathedral in Washington DC next to her teacher's.

Write about an aha moment in your life.

June 28

My high school superlative wasn't "most likely to succeed" or "class clown." I had earned "luckiest", though I probably should have earned "Most likely to trip on stage at graduation," since I did trip on stage at graduation, and I was the only person to do so!

Did you earn a superlative in high school? If so, write about how accurate it was and why. If not, what superlative could you have earned in your opinion? What receipts do you have to support your idea?

June 29

In a *New York Times* article titled "To fall in love with anyone, do this" written by Mandy Len Catron, she describes how psychologist Arthur Aron was able to make two complete strangers fall in love by having them answer questions that became more and more personal. This set of questions is known around the internet as the "36 Questions to Fall in Love".

One question I borrowed from this list and asked during almost every first date I ever went on was, "What would constitute a 'perfect' day for you?" What surprised me most about this question was how *my* answer would always be different, even if just a little bit.

Today, write what would constitute a "perfect" day for you. Then, write yourself a reminder to answer this question again in one year's time. How are the two similar or different? Are there surprising changes?

June 30

On June 30, 2022, Ketanji Brown Jackson, was sworn in as the first-ever Black female supreme court justice in the United States. In her remarks she made after her nomination was confirmed the previous April, she said "I am... ever buoyed by the leadership of generations past who helped to light the way. Dr. Martin Luther King Jr., Justice Thurgood Marshall, and my personal heroine, Judge Constance Baker Motley. They and so many others did the heavy lifting that made this day possible."

Write about the people, perhaps personal heroes or heroines, who have done the "heavy lifting" that has allowed you to achieve a moment of success or even be able to do something quotidian.

July 1

The first book I ever read that made me cry was Stephen Chbosky's novel *The Perks of Being a Wallflower* about an introverted teen struggling to find belonging and to navigate the world with undiagnosed PTSD. In one scene, as the main character, Charlie, rides in a car with his friends listening to David Bowie, he remarks, "And in that moment, I swear we were infinite".

Write about a time you felt infinite, or as poet Li-Young Lee put it in his poem "From Blossoms", "as if death were nowhere / in the background".

July 2

Today is "Halfway Day," the *official* halfway point in the calendar year. Many who observe Halfway Day see it as a second New Year; a day to reevaluate how the year is going and decide what changes need to be made.

For this writing prompt, write something halfway. Don't make any notes to yourself about how you want it to end. Just let it sit in your journal or on your computer. Make a note to yourself in your calendar to return to your writing and finish it at the end of the year. (Don't worry, I'll remind you too.)

July 3

Branching off of "Halfway Day," now is the perfect time to experiment with "Creative Cross-Training." Athletes often cross-train, or exercise in a method outside their normal regimen in order to develop their overall fitness and prevent injuries or overuse. For example, long distance runners may cross-train with lower impact cardio workouts like biking or swimming. Similarly, creatives can "cross-train" by experimenting with different artistic endeavors.

Are you a poet? Try your hand at watercolors. Are you a painter? Challenge yourself to create a dance choreography. An actor? Grab some clay (or Play-Doh) and sculpt. It doesn't matter if you have "talent" in these other fields. The purpose is the process not the product.

Afterward, you can think about what you learned from the experience. Can you use your "cross-training" in your regular métier?

July 4

Araminta Ross, known now by her self-given name Harriet Tubman, is infamous for risking her own life and freedom, after having escaped enslavement, to lead dozens of enslaved people from the southern United States to freedom in the north via the Underground Railroad, and her heroism did not end there. She was also the first woman to ever coordinate and lead a military assault in US history. During the Civil War, she led a regiment of soldiers on an operation in Combahee Ferry, SC that forced confederate soldiers to retreat and resulted in the freeing of over 700 enslaved people. About her motivation to risk her life to save others she is quoted by Sarah Bradford as saying, "I had crossed the line. I was free; but there was no one to welcome me to the land of freedom... to this solemn resolution I came; I was free, and they should be free also; I would make a home for them in the North, and the Lord helping me, I would bring them all there."

In today's writing, reflect on freedom and the ways in which people around the world are still trying to reach it.

July 5

I'll always remember my high school art teacher, Ms. Quinn. For one project, I created a three-foot by two-foot collage. I cut out a model's face from the cover of a magazine, tore it in half, and pasted it at the bottom of my canvas. Coming out of the split halves, I pasted a clutter of images including bathroom scales, depictions of war, angry and sad faces, and the like. When Ms. Quinn chose the piece to be in the school art show, I was hesitant to have my name displayed next to something so vulnerable. She told me that art should elicit a feeling in the viewer, and that those feelings don't always have to be positive. She added that other students who might be feeling similarly but too scared to say so, might see the work and feel less alone.

Write about the teacher who had the biggest impact on your life, whether it was from a formal school setting or otherwise.

July 6

Jeffrey Marsh is a nonbinary writer, artist, activist, and social media influencer, best known for making viral videos focused on encouragement, self-love, and LGBTQIA+ celebration. During their book launch party for *Take Your Own Advice,* a fan told them that she was fully estranged from her abusive mother, but finds that sometimes she deeply misses her. Jeffrey's suggestion? If this fan knows the best thing for her is to maintain zero contact, then in the moments when she is missing her mom, she can work to embody the qualities that she misses. Does her mom make the greatest meatballs? The fan can work on her own recipe. Did her mom have an angelic singing voice? The fan could take voice lessons herself. In doing so, even if her meatballs never reached the same level as her mother's, she would be taking active steps to empower herself.

Write about someone you miss. What qualities of theirs do you admire? In which ways can you embody their qualities yourself?

July 7

Karon Davis is an acclaimed American sculptor who uses a unique plaster method to create both life-sized and larger-than-life-sized works that often depict individuals in the midst of dance or performance.

According to her biography on the Wilding Cran Gallery website, her use of white plaster strips in her sculptures stems from her "longtime interest in ancient Egyptian mummification practices" that used "wrapping to memorialize different bodies and their complex histories."

In today's writing, memorialize (in other words, create something that serves as a reminder or tribute of) different bodies. Perhaps you consider the ways in which your own body has changed and its complex histories throughout your life. Or perhaps you memorialize an array of different bodies that have had an impact on you. What about these different bodies do you want to ensure is never forgotten?

July 8

A former partner of mine loved the British comedy series The IT Crowd. I never watched it with him, but regularly heard quips since he would watch the series all the way through to the end, just to start it over from the beginning again. In one scene, the character Moss addresses his co-worker Roy, saying, "I thought you hated parties." Roy corrects him saying that he likes parties, but hates balloons [that are typically found at parties]. Roy goes on to explain, "They explode suddenly, and unexpectedly. They are filled with the capacity to give me a little fright, and I find that unbearable."

And I have never felt more seen. I *hate* balloons. One time I was asked as an ice breaker question, "Where's a place you could hide that no one would look to find you?" and I answered "A balloon factory".

Write about a time when a book, film, TV series, song, or other media made you feel seen and understood.

July 9

If you've ever participated in a production of William Shakespeare's *Macbeth,* then you are probably familiar with the superstition that bars anyone from saying the play's title within a theater's walls, often using the euphemism "The Scottish play" to reference it instead. The superstition may have begun because of the witches involved in the play, believing that Shakespeare used actual witch spells in his script, which caused the play to be cursed.

In today's writing, include a superstition that you have or that you know of.

July 10

Named after the tennis champion who became the first Black man to win singles titles at the US Open, the Australian Open, and Wimbledon, Arthur Ashe Stadium is the tennis arena currently used for the US Open and is the largest tennis arena in the world.

Ashe is credited with saying, "From what we get, we can make a living; what we give, however, makes a life."

Write about the ways you give. How does this giving shape your life?

July 11

When thinking about the grizzly bear, images of the brown beasts parked in rivers eating fish they plucked out of the water, or climbing trees to have at the honey within a beehive, or mauling tourists in Yellowstone National Park might come to mind. The first thing you think of is probably not that they can eat upwards of 40,000 moths a day! That's right, *moths.*

In the spring and summer months as bears emerge from their winter torpor, the cutworm moth migrates from the northern regions of Canada to the Rocky Mountain West by the hundreds of millions, and are sometimes referred to as "bear butter" because they act as such good sources of fat for the griz populations in Wyoming and Montana.

Write about something that might be surprising for someone to learn about *you*.

July 12

Have you ever experienced "love at first sight"? It has only happened to me once. When I first moved to Western New York, I was living in a dormitory with a communal dining hall. My first morning having breakfast with the other people living on campus, I was introduced to a woman, and when I looked at her, I was immediately overcome with emotion. I blushed and had to look away for fear everyone, but especially she, would notice my embarrassing reaction. My heart rattled like a jackhammer, and I was struck by this feeling like, "Oh my god, I am so in love with this person who I don't even know."

We ended up dating, and there's not enough room on this page to go into the details, but the TL;DR version is it turned out to be the most toxic, emotionally abusive relationship I have ever been in to this day. (And obviously I've healed and am no longer bitter about it...)

Write about a time your heart betrayed you.

July 13

Renowned Mexican painter, Frida Kahlo, began painting while recovering from the many medical operations she endured after a metal handrail impaled her pelvis and abdomen during a bus accident when she was only 18 years old. She used the creative outlet as a means of processing both her physical and emotional pain following the crash.

In her portrait "The Two Fridas", a lighter-skinned version of herself wearing a European-style wedding dress holds hands with a darker-skinned version of herself wearing Tehuana clothing. The two figures have exposed anatomical hearts which attach to one another. These two Fridas may represent her Hungarian-German heritage from her father's side and her Spanish-Indigenous-Mexican heritage from her mother's side and how those cultures impacted her self-image and her interactions with others including her then-husband.

Today, write "The Two [insert your name]s". Who are these individuals? How do they work with or against each other?

July 14

Happy "Be Nice to Bugs" Day! Steven Kutcher worked in Hollywood for years as the go-to "Bug Man." According to his website, "His knowledge of arachnids and their behavior led him to work with arthropods on over 80 feature films including *Arachnophobia*, *Jurassic Park*, and *Spider-Man*." When CGI started to replace him, he began painting... using his bugs instead of brushes... He'd put paint on the bottoms of their feet and let them crawl around his canvases, creating a work of art from the patterns his bug pals left behind.

For this prompt, write about bugs! Can you incorporate a trail of footprints into your piece?

July 15

The Mi'kmaq are a First Nations people of Canada's Atlantic Provinces as well as northeastern Maine. To avoid encounters with sharks while traveling by water craft, the Mi'kmaq traditionally tied eelgrass and spruce tree roots to their boats, letting the plants dangle in the water. Rather than seeing the small boats as potential prey, the sharks are able to taste the natural oils from the plants that leach into the water and are put off, thinking they are swimming closer to the shore than they actually are. After all, a beached shark is almost certainly a dead shark.

Write about the tactics you employ—either consciously or subconsciously—to thwart the metaphorical sharks in your life.

July 16

Will Ferrell is an actor known across the globe for his outlandish characters starting most notably with the weekly comedy sketch show, Saturday Night Live.

In 2024, he launched a documentary titled *Will & Harper* which followed him and his best friend as they traveled across the country together after Harper came out as a trans woman. At the end of the movie, the song "Harper and Will Go West" is performed by Kristen Wiig in which she sings, ♫ *A friend is a friend is a friend till the end* ♫

Write about a friend who has witnessed you in more than one chapter of your life. Who were you when you first met? Who were they? Who are you now? Who are they now? How can your friendship be described in terms of "there and then" and "here and now"?

July 17

Douglas Ridloff is a Deaf poet and founder of Deaf Poets Society who performs his poetry in American Sign Language (ASL) and visual vernacular (a storytelling technique that uses mime, body postures, and facial expressions to convey a message or feeling). Even though he cannot hear them, he has even collaborated with musicians who have composed musical scores to accompany his visual poetry performances.

While giving a TEDx Talk in Vienna, he shared that growing up, he didn't know ASL could be used artistically and not just as a practical means of communication. Now his mission is to share his visual poetry with Deaf and hearing communities all over the world so that people can better understand ASL's richness and complexity.

Today, let's experiment. Using a piece of your own writing or someone else's work that calls to you, allow yourself the freedom to create a physical visualization of that work.

July 18

In her book *Writing Toward Home*, author and poet Georgia Heard, encourages her readers to fall in love every day with the world. In fact, she suggests falling in love *at least* three times a day and allowing that feeling of falling in love to open one's heart and mind.

Get ready to fall in love! Make it a point to fall in love at least three times today. Each time you fall in love with the way the sun creates a neon lining around a cloud, or with the aroma wafting from your favorite cafe, or with the sight of your front door after a long day of work, take a minute or two to make note of it. What is it about this moment that elicited the feeling?

July 19

I'm not a sports girly, so when out with friends who are watching a game, I usually root for the team whose mascot or uniforms I like the best, especially if they're red—my favorite color.

As it turns out, according to a study that was published in the *Journal of Sports Sciences*, red-colored uniforms are associated with long-term team success! (At least in soccer.) It's not due to higher visibility since teams with equally high visibility uniforms like bright yellow did not have the same effect. Rather, some psychologists believe the correlation stems from the color's impact on self-perception since red is often associated with aggression or intensity. Athletes wearing red, then, have a subconscious mental advantage.

Before you write today, if you have anything red—a t-shirt, dress, swimsuit, lipstick, wig, whatever!—put it on. Look at yourself in the mirror with this red on. (If you don't have anything red, try just imagining yourself in something red.) Then, after a good head-to-toe gander, start writing.

July 20

Happy Birthday to me! In addition to being the day the Apollo 11 mission landed on the moon in 1969, I share this birthday with actor Omar Epps, model Gisele Bündchen, actress Sandra Oh, musician Carlos Santana, and fitness guru Cathe Friedrich.

Look up the celebrities who were born on your birthday and write about what a joint birthday party with one of them would be like.

July 21

In her book *All About Love: New Visions*, bell hooks wrote that "the most precious gift true love offers [is] the experience of knowing we always belong."

Write about what "belonging" means to you. When, where, and/or with whom have you felt like you truly belonged?

July 22

Goosebumps, or the physiological response of body hair standing on end, is believed to be vestigial from when our simian ancestors had much more hair/fur covering their bodies. When hairs stand on end, a layer of air becomes trapped close to the body. That air is heated by body heat and then acts as an insulating layer.

When goosebumps appear because of an intense feeling like fear or surprise, it's like when a scared cat puffs up its fur. It's another vestigial reaction from a time when looking larger and more intimidating to a predator, competitor, or other threat could mean the difference between life and death.

We have goosebumps when we experience awe or love too because those emotions are connected to the same parts of our brain that govern our "fight or flight" response.

Write about the last time you experienced goosebumps. Were you cold? Scared? Or overcome with emotion?

July 23

One of the wildest spelled words in the English language, in my opinion, is the word zhuzh. Like, when you give your hair a little zhuzh with some hair spray. Or when you zhuzh up a boring outfit with a snappy piece of jewelry. When pronounced, zhuzh sounds like there should be a "j" in it somewhere, but alas, no "j".

The word originates in Polari, a kind of secret code language made up of English and Cockney slang, Italian, and Romani, that was used by street and circus performers, but was particularly a part of gay culture in the UK when homosexuality was against the law. The word "polari" is likely an anglicized adaptation of the Italian word "parlare" meaning "to speak."

Think of a word that you love the sound of or that you think is utterly ridiculous. Research the etymology of the word, and use those origins to inspire your writing today. Imagine the first person who uttered this word. Who were they? Where did they live? What was the context in which they said this word?

July 24

The cactus-like plants that grow in the southwestern United States and northern Mexico called Joshua trees are neither cacti nor trees. They are actually in the asparagus family! Poison ivy? Not in the ivy family, but in the cashew family. Or how about clovers, those typically tri-leafed plants associated with Ireland, they are in the pea family!

Write about the people who are surprisingly a part of your family. What about them stands out as unexpected?

July 25

Have you ever had a great idea while in the shower? Or maybe you have heard of this phenomenon happening to someone else? Well, there might be some science behind it. Taking a warm shower increases the flow of dopamine in the body, which supports the parts of the brain responsible for creativity.

Today, take a warm shower before sitting down to write. Take your time while in the shower. Give the muse time to visit you as you wash behind your ears.

July 26

A "big fish story" is an over-the-top and exaggerated tale that is likely untrue. Big fish stories are usually told while bragging about an accomplishment or experience, the way anglers often exaggerate how big of a fish they caught.

Today, revisit a piece of writing and turn it into a big fish story. For example, if in the text, the weather is drizzly, revise it so that there was a thunderstorm or hurricane. Or if someone is wearing a suit jacket, revise it so they are wearing a full tuxedo. If a car was making a weird clicking sound, revise it so that the car was moments from completely breaking down. If someone was annoyed by something, send them into a flying rage. If they smiled softly, make them giddy with glee. No matter how minor, try to transform each detail into hyperbole.

July 27

When I was in college, I was cast as "The Woman Who Loved to Make Vaginas Happy" in the university's production of *The Vagina Monologues* written by V, formerly known as Eve Ensler. My character was a lesbian, dominatrix sex worker, and I dressed the part; I felt so empowered to don the persona of someone so sexually free. The day of the play's premiere, I got food poisoning and spent the entire evening queasy. Instead of letting anyone know, I tried to push through, but then in the middle of my monologue, I started feeling light-headed. I ran off stage and fainted. When I woke, I was covered in vomit. Someone called 9-1-1 which triggered the campus police to come. The rest of the night was a fiasco as I was carted off to the emergency room to receive IV fluids. I should have just stayed home and let an understudy take my place, but NoOoOoOo. In my mind, the show had to go on!

Write about a time when stubbornness got the best of you or someone you know.

July 28

One artwork that I return to again and again is Pamela Phatsimo Sunstrum's Quadra IV. When I look at it, I see a person in movement, perhaps who has stumbled, but won't let the stumble stop their momentum. I see a starry night sky. A piece of fabric in a geometric pattern drapes across the person and under their feet, but it could also be a map or representative of the earth itself.

Write about a work of art that has captivated you in the past. When did you first see it? Why do you think it has such a hold on you?

July 29

All across the world, human beings have participated in wedding ceremonies to inanimate objects. A man from Indonesia married a rice cooker. A woman from the United States married a roller coaster. A man from Korea married a video game character. A woman from India married a tree. A man from China married a robot he built himself.

Write about your hypothetical wedding to an inanimate object. How did you know it was true love? What would be included in your vows?

July 30

When my husband and I conceived our son, it was after months of trying. I had just turned 37, and I struggled with severe anxiety each time we *tried* because I felt the immense pressure of hoping for success. The last time we tried, as I wept and begged the Universe, "Please, please, please," a clap of thunder rattled our studio apartment. My husband playfully said, "Is that you, Baby?", and my next pregnancy test was positive.

When I was massively pregnant, I had an induction scheduled for a Friday morning. The Tuesday night before, as my husband and I were going to bed, a lightning bolt lit our room up like a camera flash before we heard the thunder roll. Jokingly I said, "Do you think that's the baby saying he's on his way?" Sure enough, a couple hours later, I was at the hospital. My water had broken.

In today's writing include a clap of thunder that signals a big change.

July 31

In part of her book *Braiding Sweetgrass*, Robin Wall Kimmerer wrote about canoe camping in the Adirondacks with her family: "Most summer mornings of childhood I woke to the sound of the outhouse door—the squeak of the hinge followed by the hollow *thunk* as it shut." She then went on to recount her father's morning coffee ritual, how he would pour coffee into the earth before pouring any for himself or her mother, saying "Here's to the gods of Tahawus."

Today, begin your writing with the phrase "Most summer mornings of childhood I woke to the sound of..." and then let the writing flow from there.

August 1

Today marks the beginning of the annual Sealey Challenge. Invented by poet Nicole Sealey, the challenge dares participants to read one poetry collection each day in the month of August. Try as I might, as of this writing, I have yet to complete this challenge. BUT! The beauty of challenges like this is even if I don't complete the challenge 100%, I still reap the benefits of completing it 90% or 50% or even 10%. If I read one extra book that I wouldn't have otherwise because of this challenge, that is still an overall positive.

Write about something you've been trying to do FoReVeR, but just can't manage to cross the finish line. In which ways is the effort of trying still benefiting you even if you haven't yet reached your goal?

August 2

In his poem "Feet" from his collection *Catalog of Unabashed Gratitude*, Ross Gay opens with "Friends, mine are ugly feet". The poem goes on to describe the moment when a friend told the speaker "you have pretty feet." The speaker later, as if giving up on writing a poem and just wanting to be frank with the reader, recounts how that friend passed away from leukemia, and really they were trying to write a poem about that sweet person and all of the emotion and memory that went into one brief compliment.

Write about a compliment you will never forget.

August 3

Hugh Everett III is associated with the idea of a "multi-verse", theorizing that every quantum event (or a phenomenon that occurs at the subatomic level) causes the universe to split apart into a new version of itself leading to an infinitesimal number of universes that are disconnected from one another. Sci-fi films depicting this idea include *Spider-Man: Into the Spider-Verse, Everything Everywhere All at Once, The One*, and more.

Write about what the you in another universe might be like. What is the universe like there?

August 4

When baseball shortstop, Trea Turner, was first signed to the Philadelphia Phillies, he struggled to meet performance expectations, batting below average at .235. To show their disapproval, disappointed fans started booing him whenever he would go up to bat.

A campaign soon spread to give Turner a standing ovation the next time he went up to home plate instead of booing, and the campaign was successful. Not only did fans show Turner love, his batting average went up to .337, and he set a record for most bases stolen without being caught.

Write about a person who might benefit from some extra encouragement.

August 5

Many people, particularly those who practice Judeo-Christian religions, know of The Ten Commandments. The American Humanist Association presents a parallel set of guiding principles called The Ten Commitments: empathy, critical thinking, responsibility, ethical development, global awareness, peace & social justice, environmentalism, service & participation, humility, and altruism. Instead of "Thou shall not", these commitments use "I will" language. For example, "Altruism: I will help others in need without hoping for rewards."

Write about the principles that inform your sense of right and wrong.

August 6

In poet Danez Smith's poem "broke n rice", they begin with praise for the food, its seasonings, and pairings, but then further down in the poem, the speaker admits to having hated it before because of its connection to poverty: "h ated the w ate r / gh ostbl eac hed by sta rc h / hat ed th e p uff y mo on s / po ckin g my sto m a ch".

(If you notice, the added blank spaces within the words create a visual effect as if the poem itself were composed of rice grains.)

But then the speaker turns away from those former feelings, expressing that they "hat ed ev eryth ing/ th at i woul d mar ry no w".

Write about something you hated when you were younger but now love. What caused your change of heart?

August 7

The mimic octopus is the mockingbird of the sea. Though, instead of imitating sounds, the mimic octopus manipulates its body to resemble other animals such as sea snakes, jellyfish, and flatfish to elude predators.

Today, mimic a genre of writing you're unused to. How would you manipulate your writing to resemble a journalist, a lyricist, a poet, a horror writer, a sitcom writer, a playwright, a technical writer, or other genre that appeals to you?

August 8

A bucket list is a list of experiences and/or achievements a person hopes to accomplish before the end of their life.

A decade after her father passed away from a collision with a distracted driver, author Laura Carney discovered her father's bucket list and began a quest to complete her father's dreams for him. She spent six years completing over 50 bucket list items and recounted her adventure in her book *My Father's List*.

Write your bucket list from ten years ago. Are there items on it that you can check off now? Once you've completed your past-self's list, expand on it to include new dreams and desires you hope to achieve before it's too late.

August 9

In 1994, the United Nations established August 9th as the International Day of the World's Indigenous Peoples. According to the UN, an estimated 476 million Indigenous peoples in the world live across 90 countries, speak 40% of the world's 7,000 languages, and represent over 5,000 different cultures. Yet, throughout history, their traditions, communities, and livelihoods have been violated, exploited, and decimated, usually in the name of "modernization" or "progress" forced upon Indigenous peoples by oppressive colonizers.

Write about something "modern" or "progressive" that has had negative consequences on society, a community, or you as an individual. What might the present world look like without this "advancement?"

August 10

In 1946, Hans Lorenzen and Sepp Reindle invented the team sport known as "goalball" specifically for athletes with vision disabilities. At the time, goalball was a way for WWII veterans who lost their sight to rehabilitate. In the mid-1970s, goalball became an official Paralympic sport and is one of only two Paralympic sports that do not have an Olympic counterpart. (The other is boccia!) To play, two teams of three players each place themselves on either side of a court the size of a volleyball court and attempt to earn points by rolling a ball containing bells along the floor into the opponent's goal which stretches across the entire width of the court. Because of the role hearing plays in the sport, spectators must remain silent while the athletes are playing. All players must wear eye masks to neutralize any differences in vision disability.

If you don't have a vision disability, close your eyes and write about what you can sense around you. Keep your eyes shut as you bring pen to paper or fingers to keyboard.

August 11

Humans and trees have more similarities than we might realize. For example, when some trees experience a stressor —an invasive insect, leaf-munching herbivore, or tree disease—they will emit chemical signals that alert the trees around them of the threat. Those trees can then prepare their defenses, like by producing a chemical to make themselves less tasty to a would-be grazer.

Humans have similar capabilities. When we sweat due to fear or anxiety, the stress hormones in our sweat subconsciously alert the people around us to be on guard for whatever potential threat is nearby.

If a tree is visible from your writing space, observe its trunk and branches. Maybe you would even want to go outside to touch it or look more closely. If there are no trees physically near you, find a picture in a book or on the internet. After studying the tree, write about the ways in which you might relate to this living being. How are your lives similar and/or intertwined?

August 12

Blue whales are not just the largest creature on Earth, they are the largest creature to have ever lived; larger than any dinosaur we have evidence of. Their hearts alone weigh around 400 lbs (180 kg). Their deep vocalizations, that are louder than jet engines, can travel up to 1,000 miles (1,600 km) through the water. These vocalizations help them to keep track of one another when migrating, warn each other about potential threats, and woo each other during mating season. Though their songs seem to follow some generalized patterns, researchers have found that males will often "improvise" when in a group similar to when band members exchange riffs. This interaction isn't competitive the way some song birds trill back and forth to establish territory or assert dominance, rather the whales are solidifying social connections.

Write about a time you sang with loved ones. What song were you singing? What had brought you together before the sing-along?

August 13

While going through chemotherapy, the renowned poet Andrea Gibson, recounted in their newsletter "Things That Don't Suck" that as they lost the hair all over their body, their eyebrows stayed intact. One day, their parents called to say that their father had woken up with his right eyebrow missing; just all of the hairs in the eyebrow fell out. As they concluded in their newsletter, "My father's eyebrow left his face so my eyebrows wouldn't leave mine."

Whether you believe in this kind of mystical magic or not, write about a covenant that took place in the spirit world. How did it impact those living in the human world?

August 14

In British poet Harry Baker's poem "Paper People," he takes the concept of alliteration to new heights. He creates a world of "proper pop-up purple paper people," imagining what this world might look like with their "paper people politics" and their "pompous paper parliament." He also incorporates elements of our modern culture joking that "there'd be a paper Princess Kate but we'd all stare at paper Pippa," referencing the UK's Princess of Wales and her sister.

In today's writing, choose a letter or sound and include it as much as you can throughout your text.

August 15

Do you have a nemesis poem/novel/idea? Something that you have been trying to write about for ages, but for some reason your attempts keep falling short? For me, as of this writing, I keep trying (and failing) to write about this one time when my husband and I were on a sunset hike, and as we were walking back to our car, my husband noticed a bee asleep atop a purple aster. Then we noticed another purple aster had a bee in it, and another, and another. Lining this pathway almost every aster had a sleeping bee on it. The next day while researching it, I learned that bees will often sleep away from the hive when they know they are close to death so as to not infect the hive with their corpse. Every time I try to write a poem about this, it just doesn't come out right.

Do you have a nemesis idea? Take a stab at it again today. If not, wanna take a stab at *my* nemesis? Write something about the bees sleeping in the flowers and how they know they're close to death. Oh, dear God, if it can't be me, please, someone, write this poem.

August 16

In an interview with Marion Roach Smith, spoken word poet Megan Falley said, "[M]y earliest wound that defined a trajectory of my life was being looked at and being criticized... And I do think even my love for performance has been a demand to be seen and to be loved."

Write about the ways you try to be seen and/or loved.

August 17

During the summer between my first and second years of graduate school, I worked at an organic rice farm/bird sanctuary in exchange for room and board. While there, I helped local ecologists place ID bands on flamingo chicks' ankles so they could track the flock's population size, migrations, overall community health, and more.

I was handed a fluffy gray chick (they're not born pink!) with its legs folded up, and I held its body with its wings tucked as if it were a football. As I watched the other volunteers, I saw scrawny gray necks snaking around and snapping at arms and hands with their beaks. No one reacted to these little nips, but I was still not keen to receive one! Inevitably, as I held my chick, its beak pecked my arms and hands, and I discovered that it, in fact, did not hurt at all. It felt more like the flamingo was giving me a little kiss!

Write about something that you feared until you experienced it and realized you had nothing to fear in the first place.

August 18

Dating and relationship coach, Traci Porterfield, recommends DSD or "doing something different" when stuck in a rut. She says "When you have a desire for change in your life, you want to feel differently, to feel happier, to attract more love or success, the easiest way to get momentum is with a little 'DSD.'"

Today, DSD. If you normally write on your computer, then write longhand. If you normally write with a pen, write with a child's crayon or tube of lipstick. If you normally write stream of consciousness, write a poem. If you normally write inside at a desk, go outside. If you normally listen to indie folk music while you write, listen to death metal. Just DSD!

August 19

When planting beans, my green bean farmer friend told me that planting them in dry soil forces the beans to grow more robust roots because they have to search deeper for water. This effort makes them more likely to survive the varying weather conditions of the growing season. However, if they are planted in wet soil, the roots don't have to go very far to find water, making them more shallow and more susceptible to the elements.

Write about the efforts you have exerted to better secure your future. What is your equivalent of searching for water in dry soil?

August 20

The children's book *The Man Who Didn't Like Animals* by Deborah Underwood and illustrated by LeUyen Pham, tells the story of a city man who lived alone in a clean and animal-free home until a cat appeared on his door step. The man tells the cat to go away, but the cat decides to stay. The man doesn't like this initially, but then grows to enjoy the cat's company. Then another cat arrives. Then a dog. Then another dog. Then ducks and chickens. Then goats and pigs and cows until his neighbors give him an ultimatum that leads the man to ask all the animals to leave. As he watches them process away, he runs after them, deciding he's going to leave his home in the city to live with the animals in the countryside. The story ends "And that's how it all began" with an illustration of the man painting "Old MacDonald's Farm" on an archway sign as the animals sing "EE-I-EE-I-O" around an upright piano.

In today's writing, think of a story or nursery rhyme, and write about what happened *before* the story we currently know.

August 21

You might be familiar with the concept of the five "Love Languages" theorized by the author and marriage counselor Gary Chapman. They include words of affirmation, quality time, receiving gifts, acts of service, and physical touch. Well, I theorize the five *Hate* Languages: the things people do that make us feel like they just don't care. My Love Language is quality time, so my *Hate* Language is *wasted* time. When people show up late or don't show up at all with no reasonable explanation, that is like the ultimate Hate Language to me. Or if I am out with someone, and they spend the whole time on their phone. If I show up on time and am giving my time to *them* when I am a busy woman with a million other things going on, then I want that reciprocated.

Write about your Love and Hate Languages.

August 22

In A. Van Jordan's poetry collection, *M-A-C-N-O-L-I-A*, which engages with the story of MacNolia Cox who was the first African American to reach the final round of the American national spelling bee at age thirteen, Jordan uses the style of a dictionary definition as the vessel for some of his poems.

Explore this idea of the dictionary definition. Maybe you want to write a definition of your own name. Or a word you have been labeled as. Or perhaps you want to choose a word at random from a book on your shelf and create an artistic interpretation of its meaning.

August 23

In psychologist Mihály Csíkszentmihályi's widely-cited books *Flow* and *Finding Flow*, he posits that "flow" in essence is a psychological state in which we experience uninterrupted focus and enjoyment while performing an activity. It's a state so deep that one often loses track of time and their sense of self. This deep state can feel meditative and rejuvenating.

To achieve "flow", he theorizes that four criteria need to be met: 1. The activity cannot be too easy or too difficult; 2. The activity has a clear goal and feedback to ensure the goal is on its way to being met; 3. Distractions need to be eliminated including one's own self-consciousness; and 4. The activity needs to feel enjoyable or rewarding in some way.

Write about when you have experienced flow with your art. In which ways were each of these criteria met at the time to allow you to achieve the flow state?

August 24

In the late 19th century, a tiny aphid-like insect that feeds on grapevine roots was ravaging French vineyards. French botanist, Pierre Viala, knew the solution was to find a species of grape that was resistant to this pest, and then breed the species together. His search brought him to none other than the state of Texas. With help from Texan botanist Thomas Munson, the team brought tens of thousands of Texan grapevine rootstocks to France where they then grafted the roots to French grapevine species. This process saved the French wine industry from annihilation.

The next time you're enjoying a Chardonnay or Bordeaux (or NA versions for non-drinkers), you can say Yee-haw!

Write about a time you received help from an unlikely place.

August 25

Dame Antonia Susan Duffy, known professionally by her former married name as A. S. Byatt, is a British novelist, poet, short story writer, and literary critic whose books have been widely translated into more than thirty languages. In one of her essays on storytelling she wrote, "Narration is as much a part of human nature as breath and the circulation of the blood."

Write the personal story that is so ingrained in your identity that it might as well be your breath or blood.

August 26

Different species of fireflies display their bioluminescence with different frequencies as well as different lengths of glow time. It's a kind of individual communication that helps to attract mates of the correct species. However, some female firefly species use what ecologists call "aggressive mimicry", a kind of lying in the animal world. They can imitate the glow patterns of other firefly species in order to lure males to them so they can feed on them! Firefly femme fatale!

Write about a time when you (or someone else who was definitely not you since you would never do such a thing) lied in order to get what you wanted.

August 27

My sister's birthday is 8/27, and that number combination pops up in my everyday life more often than any other number combination. I catch 8:27 on the clock, I see 827 on Captchas and license plates. One time a gas station I just happened to stop at outside Joshua Tree National Park had a big advertisement for cigarettes priced at $8.27.

Psychologists might label this occurrence as a kind of cognitive bias called Frequency Illusion. My brain has become selectively attentive to this number combination, and every time I notice it, the neural pathway becomes reinforced.

Write about a number that has significant meaning to your life. Perhaps it's a lucky number or a particular date you'll always remember. Maybe it's your childhood best friend's phone number that you memorized long ago but still remember.

August 28

The urban legend that we only use 10% of our brain is completely untrue. We use our entire brains to process emotions, remember information, and perform bodily functions. However, it *is* true that only about 5% of our brain is used for conscious processing. The rest of it is subconscious or unconscious activity. Though we humans have no *conscious* memories of our infanthoods, we *do* have *subconscious* memories, and these memories can form our attachment styles, our beliefs about the world, our beliefs about ourselves, and more.

Some people believe we can tap into this subconscious mind through dreaming, hypnosis, meditation, and/or manifestation.

Today, try to get in contact with your subconscious mind. Maybe you simply want to say, "Hey, Subconscious Mind, what's up? Want to share anything with me today?" Just sit and be aware for a few minutes before taking pen to paper or fingers to keyboard.

August 29

In Jon Scieszka's children's book *The True Story of the 3 Little Pigs!*, Sciezka reimagines the classic story from the wolf's perspective. In this story, the wolf explains that he simply was asking for some sugar from his neighbors so he could bake a cake for his grandmother. And he didn't *blow* the houses made of straw and sticks down, his *sneezes* destroyed them by accident. At the brick house, the third pig refused him sugar and then insulted his grandmother which sent the wolf into a rage. The pig police came and arrested him, and from behind bars, he explains how the news coverage of the event was highly exaggerated.

Today, write from the perspective of a villain.

August 30

The first ever Internet Cat Video Festival took place in Minneapolis, Minnesota in 2012. One year, I was lucky enough to be one of the 10,000 people to watch the hour-long compilation, with some of the attendees dressed in various feline attire.

Today, watch some hilarious cat videos on the internet. When one particularly draws you in, describe the clip as if writing a scene in a play or film. You might consider how this scene might fit into a larger narrative.

August 31

Sir George Ivan Morrison, aka Van Morrison, is most famously known for his 1967 classic hit "Brown Eyed Girl" which topped the charts when he was only 22 years old. Even though he has since produced over forty albums, was knighted by Queen Elizabeth II for his contributions to music, and won countless awards, he is still best known for his signature tune. In an interview with *Time Magazine,* Morrison himself said of the song: "I've got about 300 other songs I think are better than that."

Write about something you accomplished early in life. What have you gone on to achieve since then? How was this achievement a moment or a monument in your life?

September 1

One-star reviews can be at the same time infuriating as they are hilarious. When negative reviewers come for our work, it might feel like a slap in the face to the effort we put into creating our manuscript. On the other hand, some believe one-star reviews are inevitable and treat them the way that some celebrities treat "mean tweets:" sharing them as a way to poke fun at themselves and to show that negative reviews won't keep them from creating.

Write a one-star review for your own work. As Audre Lorde once wrote, "Nothing I accept about myself can be used against me to diminish me."

September 2

In one of her Substack newsletters on freelancing, poet and editor Ginger Ayla wrote, "My favorite place to be is the middle of a sentence."

Write about your favorite place to be either literally or figuratively.

September 3

Around this time of year, primary school students in the US head back to school, and to get there, many travel in a 45-foot (~14 meter) long school bus with its own distinct color: "National School Bus Glossy Yellow."

Before being standardized in 1939, children in the US went to school on foot, in trucks and buses of all different colors, and in horse-drawn wagons. Often, the mode of transportation depended on the wealth of the school district and whether it could afford transportation for its students.

Not only did the uniform color and design improve safety because the buses carrying children became more easily recognizable, costs for schools lowered because the buses could be mass-produced instead of specially made.

Write about how you went to and from school. Did you take a bus or other transport? Were you alone or with others? Was the experience enjoyable or not so much?

September 4

Takotsubo Cardiomyopathy is sometimes called "Broken Heart Syndrome." After an acute stress, like the loss of a loved one, the heart can inflame, taking on the shape of a "Takotsubo," the Japanese word for "octopus trap." If not treated immediately, the condition can lead to a fatal heart attack. One can quite literally die of a broken heart.

Write about when your heart felt the most broken. What would you tell someone who experienced the same thing you did?

September 5

In 2023, a University of California, Berkeley graduate student named Bill Zhou decided to commute via passenger plane to the Bay Area from his home in LA in order to attend classes for his year-long Master's program. He said he had a great deal on his apartment, and didn't want to have to break his lease just to live somewhere else for a year. He took a total of 238 flights over the course of the academic year. He'd have to wake up at 3:30 AM to catch a 6:00 AM flight from LAX to SFO in order to make it to his 10:00 AM classes. After attending classes all day, he'd return to LA, arriving at his home around midnight. He used frequent flier miles and spent just shy of $2,500 on flights. Based on the average cost of renting a room in a shared apartment in San Francisco in 2022-2023, Bill saved at least $7,000 in rent by commuting via plane.

Write about your commute. Even if you work from home, write about the journey to your work space. What surprising elements might you notice if you're paying particular attention to each detail?

September 6

In his poem "How to Love Your Introvert", Kevin Yang lists the hypothetical steps needed to be taken to love an introvert and includes how to tell if someone is an introvert and common misconceptions of introverts. He begins with 1, and works his way through the list, 2, 3, and so on.

Write a list of steps of how someone should properly love you. What special instructions might be helpful for their success?

September 7

In 1900, a French toymaker named Armand Gervais commissioned artist Jean-Marc Côté to design postcard-sized images that would depict what life would be like in the year 2000. In one image, students are sitting at a table with wires connected to their heads. To the side, a teacher puts books into a kind of giant meat grinder-looking contraption. Another picture shows an audience looking in awe at a horse on a stage. Yet another shows an aristocratic household sitting around a radiumplace instead of a fireplace.

Jumping further than Côté, take your writing to the year 3000. What does school look like? What does work look like? What does entertainment look like? What does everyday family time look like?

September 8

In her book *A Tree Grows in Brooklyn,* Betty Smith wrote about the protagonist Francie Nolan, "Books became her friends and there was one for every mood. There was poetry for quiet companionship. There was adventure when she tired of quiet hours. There would be love stories when she came into adolescence, and when she wanted to feel a closeness to someone she could read a biography. On that day when she first knew she could read, she made a vow to read one book a day as long as she lived."

Write about the books or other inanimate objects that could be likened to friends of yours.

September 9

In her blog post titled "On Doing What Scares You," best-selling author, Dani Shapiro wrote, "There isn't a day when I sit down to write that I am not afraid. Oh, this fear can disguise itself... it can look like resistance, or exhaustion, or distraction, or despair. It can even look like online shopping. But what it is, really—bottom line—is the fear that I won't be able to pull it off. Whatever vision exists in my mind, whatever perfect iteration of an idea, will never be achieved. So why bother? Why even try?"

Write about how your life might be different if you acted with courage rather than waiting to build up confidence. What project is being kept on the back burner? What conversation hasn't been had? What change has been pushed back time and again?

September 10

Mary Oliver started her iconic poem, "The Summer Day," with the question "Who made the world?" and ended the poem with the famous question that adorns coffee mugs, t-shirts, daily planners, and decorative canvases on bedroom walls across the globe: "Tell me, what is it you plan to do / with your one wild and precious life?"

Start and end today's writing with a question.

September 11

Most Americans who were born and have memories before 2001 have a "where were you on 9/11" story.

I was sitting in high school chemistry in Upstate New York when the principal came on the PA system to tell us what had happened. Classes were immediately paused, and we all stayed glued to TV screens watching live broadcasts until it was time to go home.

One of the many details that still haunt me is hearing the final voicemail messages the victims left for their loved ones.

Imagining you only had a few minutes to share one last message with someone you loved, write what you would want them to know.

September 12

For the longest time the French film *Amélie* was my favorite movie of all-time. I have seriously seen it over 200 times since it debuted in 2001. I cut my hair like hers, I learned to speak French, and I even became a foreign exchange student to France when I was in high school because I wanted to *be* Amélie.

Not too long ago, though, I watched the film again for the first time in a long time, and I was surprised to find it was rather *cringey.*

In one scene, the title character is seen grabbing an elderly, Blind man by the arm and leading him through a busy sidewalk describing everything she saw. The scene was portrayed as an act of kindness, but we would call that ableist saviorism now. Additionally, Amélie makes a duplicate key to the antagonist's home and alters things while he is at work so that he believes he is going insane. Eek! Amélie! That's gaslighting, chérie!

Write about something that hasn't aged well.

September 13

September 13th is National Bald is Beautiful Day! According to a study by Harvard scientists that was published in *JAMA Dermatology* in 2021, nearly one-third of survey respondents reported that people with bald heads were "unattractive" and looked "sick" like a razed cityscape, a clear cut forest, or barren desert. Excuse me, what? Hell no! Jason Statham? Gorgeous. Jada Pinkett Smith? Immaculate. And my personal favorite bald beauty (other than my husband!), the professional wrestler Cesaro. *swoon*

Write about what is beautiful in its barrenness, elegant in its emptiness, and delicate in its desolation.

September 14

In a widely spread meme, Pope Leo XIV is quoted as saying, "To be called 'woke' in a world that sleeps through suffering is no insult"... except... he never said that.

The creator of the meme even admitted to using AI to create the image in the caption of the original post.

Ask an AI app (or just someone who knows you) "What's something I might say?" Use whatever phrase is generated in your writing today.

September 15

Today is National Brain Health Day and that reminds me of the acronym BRAIN for making decisions. An elaboration on the simple pro/con list, BRAIN stands for Benefits, Risks, Alternatives, Intuition (or Information), and Nothing. The first three are pretty self-explanatory. The "I" can either remind you to ask yourself what your intuition is saying and/or, what additional information you need to make the decision. Lastly, the "N" asks, what happens if you do nothing?

Write about a decision you're grappling with or have grappled with. What would happen if you applied the BRAIN framework to your decision-making process?

September 16

If you're anything like me, then you have probably practiced tsundoku either in the past or currently. In fact, you might practice without even realizing you do. Tsundoku is a Japanese term that refers to the phenomenon of buying books even when you have an abundance that haven't been read yet.

What is a book that you have been meaning to read, but has gone unread on your shelf? What has been holding you back? Why is this book of significance to you?

September 17

In one of her writerly newsletters, poet and writer Talicha J. recounted her experience with what she calls "The Writer Womps," or the disappointments we feel across our career having to do with rejection. Of course, rejection is a huge part of the writing career; you can't have a writing career without rejection, they go hand in hand. But a Writer Womp is a rejection that still stings long after the initial hurt.

Write about a Writer Womp (or other rejection) that still hurts. Why is the sting still lingering?

September 18

Yinka Shonibare is a disabled, British-Nigerian artist whose work spans paintings, sculptures, quilts, photography, filmography, ceramics, and even clothing and upholstery. When asked in an interview with Alain Elkann how he decides if an idea will become a work of art, he responded, "A project I just finished will usually create the next project... It's almost like one project is giving birth. It's the parent of another project with new ideas."

Today, take a piece of your writing at random, then create a list of ideas for projects that could stem from it. How could this piece of writing serve as the "parent" for your next project?

September 19

If you are a *New York Times* crossword fan like I am, you probably have some of the common crossword clues and answers memorized and at the ready. For example, if the clue is something like "Olympic weapon" and the answer is four letters long, I know the answer is most likely "EPÉE". If the clue is "Stock market opener" and the answer is three letters long, it is most certainly "IPO". Because I've completed the NYT crossword every day for years, and these clues reappear over and over again, I have unintentionally memorized little bits of trivia like that the inventor of the Rubik's cube's first name is "ERNO", and an ancient Greek theater is called an "ODEON".

Today, consult a crossword puzzle for inspiration. Use one of the clues and answers as the theme of your writing today.

September 20

Why is the sky blue? To answer that, you need to know that light is made up of different light waves that translate into corresponding colors: red, orange, yellow, green, blue, indigo, and violet—aka ROYGBIV. You also need to know that those waves are longest at R and shortest at V. Ok, so when these light waves reach our atmosphere, which is made up of gases and water vapor that allow us to breathe and exist on Earth, those gases in the atmosphere cause the light waves to scatter. The atmosphere scatters the shorter waves (BIV) more than the other colors, which causes our sky to appear blue. When the sun appears at a lower angle in the sky—like at sunrise and sunset—the sun's light has to travel a longer path through the atmosphere, so the longer wavelengths (RO) are the ones visible, which causes the sky to look red and orange. But guess what! On Mars it's the opposite! Its thin atmosphere scatters red light, so the sky is red during the day, and blue at sunrise and sunset!

In today's writing include the changing of the sky's color.

September 21

The Shining is a horror novel written by acclaimed author Stephen King that was later adapted into a film starring Jack Nicholson. Because King felt the film deviated way too far from his novel, he wrote a screenplay for a miniseries adaptation and then acted as its executive producer.

Write about a book you would love to see adapted to the screen. Which actors would portray the main characters? Where would it be filmed? Which elements of the story would be most important to get exactly right?

September 22

Do you have a guilty pleasure? Mine is playing Super Auto Pets on my phone. No, it doesn't have anything to do with *auto*mobiles. It's an *auto*-battler video game, and the object is to strategically build your team of "pets" and beat the opposing team. Each pet has its own unique ability and comes with its own health and offensive metrics... okay, I'm stopping myself now.

Write about your guilty pleasure, except, *erase* the guilt. Revel in your love of reality TV or smutty romance novels or whatever supposedly asinine thing it is that adds a little enjoyment to your life.

September 23

A survey conducted in 2025 by the City of London Corporation found that after experiencing a 57% increase in about two years' time, bicycling has overtaken cars as the most used form of transportation in the UK capital thanks to a number of efforts including expanded bike lanes and bike-share networks.

If you can go on a bicycle ride today, let the *riding* inspire your *writing*. If that's not possible, include a bicycle ride or a reference to a bicycle somewhere in your writing today.

September 24

When I first met my friend Lauren, I absolutely hated her. She was friends with my dorm neighbor, Kayla, in college and lived on the floor above us. She walked around in a shorty robe with fluffy little pink slippers. She could have easily starred in the movie *Legally Blonde* instead of Reese.

As I got to know her, though, I learned she was hilarious, kind, and not superficial at all like I imagined. She became one of my best friends.

I realized my problem with her was that I was threatened by how beautiful and charming she was. People gravitated to her the way I wanted people to gravitate toward me. My ill feelings were actually a reflection of my own insecurity.

Write about a time when your first impression was completely wrong.

September 25

Shel Silverstein is best known for his fantastical poetry collections *The Light in the Attic* and *Where the Sidewalk Ends*. But he was also the lyricist behind Johnny Cash's hit single "A Boy Named Sue." He even won a Grammy for Best Country Song in 1970.

The whole song, the speaker laments his name because it is traditionally feminine, and he recounts having suffered ridicule growing up because of it. Even after his father explains he named his son Sue so that he would grow up to have a thick skin, the speaker says if he has a son, he'll name him anything other than Sue.

Write the story of your name.

September 26

In 2013, a team of researchers published their article "Attractiveness of women with rectovaginal endometriosis: a case-control study" which determined that women with rectovaginal endometriosis were judged as "attractive" or "very attractive" at a higher percentage than women in two control groups.

The article was later retracted by the authors in 2020 due to the backlash they received from its publication, but not without the qualifier, "We believe that our findings have been partly misinterpreted."

What shocks me the most is that it was published in the *peer-reviewed* journal *Fertility and Sterility*, which means more than one other person had to have read the study and thought "Yup, this should go to print."

Today, write a satirical scientific study that explores a ridiculous connection: How many tomatoes people with blue eyes eat; the color toothbrush people taller than 6'5" use; or other such farcical topic.

September 27

Artist Sarah Lucas uses her work to push back humorously against society's gender stereotypes and expectations of femininity. In a photograph titled "Self Portrait with Fried Eggs", the artist sits in a chair in casual jeans and a t-shirt with a fried egg sitting on each breast.

Today, write about (at least) one gender stereotype you'd like to push back against. Bonus points if you incorporate some fried eggs.

September 28

For centuries North American Indigenous communities have planted corn, beans, and squash—known as "The Three Sisters"—in a method that is modernly called "companion farming" or "companion planting". The corn creates a trellis for the climbing beans. The beans enrich the soil with nitrogen and help the corn stay stable in high winds. The squash's broad leaves keep the soil shady which retains moisture and prevents weeds.

Write about three entities that work together in community —they can be human or non-human, living or nonliving, fictitious or real.

September 29

Author Kelly McMasters published an essay in the *New York Times* titled "Why I Write My Own Obituary Every Year." In the piece she recounts how she wrote her first obituary at age 12 when her mother was tasked with the assignment as part of her training to work in a hospice facility. Over time, she continued the practice reasoning, "Writing your obituary while you're still alive can offer clarity about your life and, mercifully, if you find something lacking, you still have time to revise."

Write your obituary. Perhaps you write in earnest, writing what would be said about you if you were to die today. Or, perhaps take a more fanciful approach. As Kelly described in her essay, she sometimes writes versions in which she imagines living to 94, earning a PhD or pilot's license, owning a second home on the coast of Ireland, or winning the lottery. Or you can try your hand at one of each.

September 30

Growing up, whenever I would be upset about something someone said or did at school, my mom would say, "The best revenge is living your best life and being happy."

On the one hand, this is good guidance since I have never felt the need to inflict harm on another person or seek revenge in any kind of violent, domineering, or malicious way. On the other hand, when I'm *not* living my best life and/or I'm miserable, then I have the added stress of feeling like my enemies are now winning because I'm failing.

Write about guidance you received from an adult in your life growing up. How was this guidance beneficial? Did the guidance cause any unintended drawbacks?

October 1

L.M. Montgomery is the mastermind behind the acclaimed *Anne of Green Gables* series which centers around Anne Shirley, who L.M. described as an eleven-year-old, red-headed, freckled-face orphan girl who is adopted by Mathew and Marilla Cuthbert, aging siblings who were originally looking to adopt a boy to help them on their family farm. In chapter 16, while marveling over the autumnal colors, Anne exclaims, "I'm so glad I live in a world where there are Octobers."

Write about what you love about October.

October 2

Speaking of *Anne of Green Gables*, *Dan in Green Gables* is a modern reimagining of the classic novel. Written by Rey Terciero and illustrated by Claudia Aguirre, in this graphic novel, the protagonist is a 15-year-old, red-headed gay boy who goes to live with his grandparents in rural Tennessee.

Today, using a classic story as inspiration, reimagine the main character as LGBTQIA+ if they aren't already. How might this identity change the storyline? How might their interactions with other characters change?

October 3

Many writers over the years have written in homage to Wallace Stevens' poem "Thirteen Ways of Looking at a Blackbird" in which he marks each vignette with a roman numeral I through XIII. Craig Santos Perez' "Thirteen Ways of Looking at a Glacier," Tony Medina's "Thirteen Ways of Looking at a Black Boy," Sophia Girol's "Thirteen Ways of Looking at an Ex" are among the many examples.

Today, write your own "Thirteen Ways of Looking at a/an [insert]". Maybe you'd like to read Wallace Stevens' poem in the bonus resources beforehand (Remember that big QR code in the beginning of the book?) Or maybe you'd rather not read it! Maybe you'd like to write freely without influence from the original. It's up to you!

October 4

Have you ever observed the kind of shadow ballet that occurs when the sun shines through the leafy crown of a tree? The ephemeral patchwork of the sun's rays and the shadows created by the tree's leaves and branches has a special name in Japanese: komorebi.

Using komorebi as inspiration, assign one entity (either an object or a person, a place, whatever you want) to represent "light" and another to represent "shadow", and write about how they might dance (either literally or figuratively) together. Bonus points for observing komorebi in the wild to further inspire your writing. (You can also find a video in the bonus materials.)

October 5

Clova Rae-Smith is a jewelry designer best known for her handcrafted jewelry for... *teeth*. She makes custom grillz using precious metals and stones. In an interview with ELLE, she said that she has her own grillz too, and "...[I]f I'm feeling bad or upset, I'll put them in and they immediately make me feel better. I've had people message me saying they've never felt this confident before. I can't really explain the effect it has."

Write about an accessory that makes you feel more confident when you wear it. Or imagine an accessory that might make you feel that way. What does the before and after, both literally and metaphorically, look like?

October 6

For well over a century, spiders have been observed "ballooning" or "kiting," a behavior by which they use wind currents to "fly." They climb to a tall height and send their gossamer threads into the air creating a kind of parachute that propels the spider anywhere from small distances to hundreds of miles away. However, researchers have recently documented spiders "ballooning" using the Earth's ionosphere—the layer of the atmosphere that is electrically charged. Tiny hairs on their bodies can sense the global electric field and the spider's silk strands can "pick up" a negative charge and travel using electrostatic repulsion. From an evolutionary perspective, this behavior can help the species disperse, but they run the risk of landing in an unfavorable environment.

Write about landing in a new land—either true-to-life or imaginary. Write about how you arrived there and why.

October 7

In an interview with NPR's Terry Gross, renowned cellist Yo-Yo Ma described learning a piece of music in college that was written by the Soviet-era Russian composer Dmitri Shostakovich who used his music as a form of resistance against the Soviet regime. Ma said, "[W]hat is interesting is code. Everybody knew... in the Soviet Union... what that music was about, and it's harder to censor notes than words. But the messages were absolutely clear... Once I understood that that was the kind of advocacy, [playing my cello] was no longer about my voice, but about my advocacy for the voices of people that didn't have voices anymore."

In today's writing, use your voice to advocate for those whose voices have been silenced.

October 8

My parents had a lot of inside jokes together. One time while visiting them, my mom casually asked my dad, "Do we have any more cereal?" and my dad responded, "I'm not sure, let me check my... *stash.*" Then my mom just erupted into laughter, leaving me with a furrowed brow wondering why that was so funny. I have a catalog of memories of more situations just like this one where they're busting out laughing over something, and I'm sitting there wondering what the hell I wasn't getting.

Write the origin story of an inside joke.

October 9

In 2016 I adopted a seven-year-old German shepherd mutt named Bella. I learned on her adoption day that she was originally named after the *Twilight* protagonist Bella Swan. Since I wasn't a particular fan of that series, I searched the internet for a namesake replacement, and I learned about the Victorian era explorer Isabella Bird. My dog went by Bella Bird after that.

Write about a pet either current or from childhood. You could even write about pet plants if you wanted. If you've never had a pet, write about an interaction you've had with any animal.

October 10

Crows are fascinating creatures whose intelligence continues to be observed and documented by ecologists. One of crows' unique behaviors includes "anting," during which crows intentionally land on an anthill and allow the colony to swarm their body. The formic acid released by the ants kills any pathogens living in the birds' feathers.

Write about a habit that from the outside might appear bizarre, but that is essential to your physical, mental, emotional, or spiritual health.

October 11

The English language is an eclectic array of etymologies stemming from Latin, Greek, French, Old Norse, German, as well as Native American languages (like the word "moose" adopted from the Eastern Abnaki people) and Asian languages (like the words "yoga" adopted from Sanskrit, "ninja" adopted from Japanese, or "ketchup" evolved from Hokkien).

Write about the people, places, and philosophies that have formed you into the eclectic array of influences you are.

October 12

The Salem Witch Trials of the late 17th century remain a lesson on what could happen when judicial bodies are led by radical theocrats. Marking the end of the trials, October 12th is Freethought Day, a day which encourages decision-making based on concrete evidence and scientific reasoning rather than fear-mongering.

Write about a time when you were falsely (or maybe rightly!) accused. If you were put on trial for the accusation, what would you say in your defense? What evidence would you put forth?

October 13

In an interview with Mayank Shekhar, Bollywood actor Ranbir Kapoor discussed how he assigns each of his characters a perfume and wears that one perfume exclusively while working on a film. He said, "I have a very strong sense of smell, so whenever I smell that fragrance, it connects me every day to that character."

If you have perfume available, put some on before you start writing today. If you don't have any perfume, take a big whiff of something fragrant—a scented candle, bathroom spray, flowers, bag of coffee, or laundry detergent. Let the scent of your chosen aroma inspire your pen.

October 14

In an interview with American journalist Anderson Cooper, comedian Stephen Colbert recounted how his father and two eldest brothers were killed in a plane crash when he was only ten years old. Of the accident, he said, "What do you get from loss? You get awareness of other people's loss, which allows you to connect with that other person, which allows you to love more deeply and to understand what it's like to be a human being, if it's true that all humans suffer."

Write about when something sad or tragic in your life connected you with another person.

October 15

Today is National Mushroom Day, and believe it or not the largest known organism in the world is a honey fungus, *Armillaria ostoyae*, which spans nearly four square miles of Malheur National Forest in eastern Oregon. When imagining a mushroom, most imagine the adorable fruiting body consisting often of a stem and cap, but this species doesn't have a giant fruiting body four square miles in size. Rather, it's the network of mycelium—all the roots and rootlets— that spread itself underground that compose the enormous fungus.

Write about the network—whether social, familial, or otherwise—that sometimes goes under the radar, but that is essential to allowing you to bear fruit and thrive.

October 16

Dutch ceramicist, Rose Schmits, created a series of pots called "Crawler Pots" which feature porcelain pots with spindly, spider-like legs. Her artist statement says that her work points to the fact that "the rules of pottery can always be broken in new and interesting ways."

Today imagine an object that is normally inanimate suddenly sprouting some legs and crawling about. What would it do? Where would it go? What rules might it break?

October 17

In his 1893 play, *An Ideal Husband,* 19th-century author Oscar Wilde wrote, "When the gods wish to punish us, they answer our prayers."

Write about a time you got exactly what you wanted and later regretted it.

October 18

In my first children's book *Mommy, Why Am I a Bird?*, a little bird wants to understand *why* she is a bird. Her mother suggests different reasons like maybe it's because you were born from an egg, maybe it's because you can sing. But with each reason, the little bird has a counter reason for why that couldn't be. "But, turtles, lizards, and snakes are born from eggs, and none of them are birds... Mommy, frogs sing and they are not birds. And humans can also sing, and they are not birds either." At the end of the story, they conclude that what makes them special and unique is that they have feathers.

In today's writing, include a conversation with a mother or mother-like figure.

October 19

In 2024, California began knocking down dams that were over a hundred years old because knocking them down was less expensive than the upgrades they needed to meet environmental standards. The removal of the dams was good news to many people including Native communities like the Yurok. Not only did the dams' removal result in the restoration of over 400 miles (640 km) of the sacred Klamath River, but this river served as the historical migratory pathway for different salmon species. The restoration of the river meant restoring fish populations that experienced large drops in numbers due to the dams as well as algal blooms and fish diseases that lingered in the dam's reservoir.

Is there a dam blocking your creativity? Write about its removal. Which teams advocated to have your creativity restored and flowing? What tools are needed for the dam's destruction? What other benefits would the surrounding communities experience from your creativity's revitalization?

October 20

In her poem "Notes For the New Administration" which first appeared in *Sligo Journal of Arts & Letters*, immigrant poet, eco-folk artist, and climate justice advocate, Neha Misra writes, "We shall need a Ministry of Poetry... We shall need a National Budget for Flowers... We shall need a Department of Artistic Affairs... We shall need a National Deep Breathing Resolution... We shall need a Bipartisan Council of Laughter and Tears... We shall need a Garden of Mourning... We shall need a Declaration of Inter-dependence."

Either referencing the suggestions from Misra's poem, or coming up with your own, address your political leaders in your writing; tell them what your community, your region, your country needs and why.

October 21

After my grandfather died when I was in high school, my relatives divvied up my grandparents' household furniture, tchotchkes, and all of what goes into making a home. The only thing I wanted was the tobacco stand my grandfather made by hand. It is a wooden cube about the size of a toaster with a little door perched on two legs. It held my grandfather's pipe, glasses, harmonica, and a little music box. As a kid, I would secretly crawl into the den where it was and open the door as quietly as I could just to take a peek inside. It smelled like musty old tobacco, and for whatever reason, the little stand felt like a mystery to me, like a box of secret treasures.

Though it's a little beat up from my many moves over the years, I still have it. I'm looking at it now as I write these words.

Write about an item you would never sell, not even for a million dollars.

October 22

One time, while briefly visiting Norwich, England, I was in a random grocery store buying some snacks and everyday items, when I suddenly heard a man's voice say, "Anne?"

My first thought was, "Whoever it is couldn't possibly be addressing me. I don't know anyone here, and no one calls me 'Anne' anymore." But when I looked up, two registers down, was a guy I had graduated high school with.

In today's writing, include finding someone or something in an unexpected place.

October 23

In an interview with NPR journalist Rachel Martin, parody musician, Weird Al Yankovic said of his 22-year-old daughter Nina, "[My wife and I] always used to say it would be great if we had a Nina at every age living in our house—just one through 22. Twenty-two Ninas. Because each one is so special and so beautiful and lovely. It's such a sense of loss when that person becomes something else—equally good—but you're missing the other person."

Write about yourself or another person at every age. If that seems a little too daunting, try starting with one sentence for each year. If something particularly inspires you in one of the years, follow that instinct and keep going.

October 24

Besides being known for his symphonic compositions that transcended class, 19th century composer Franz Liszt was also a synesthete—a person for whom one sensory stimulus is felt simultaneously through a secondary sense. For example, some people can taste certain sounds in their mouth. Others might smell different textures. Liszt had a form of synesthesia called chromesthesia; he saw colors when he heard certain sounds. Some believe this ability allowed him to soar to musical stardom, creating musical pieces that were so popular, they elicited a social frenzy known as "Lisztomania."

How might the concept of synesthesia impact your descriptive writing? Can a word smell like grapes? Can velvet sound like snoring? Revisit a piece of writing. In which ways can the senses be entangled in order to come up with completely new ways to describe common objects or occurrences?

October 25

In his book *The Creative Act*, music producer Rick Rubin suggests an exercise in which the reader sets a timer for five minutes and beats a pillow. Then once the timer goes off, he suggests immediately writing one's stream of consciousness.

Why not give his exercise a try right now?

October 26

Has anyone ever told you that the effervescent wine known as "champagne" can only be called "champagne" if the grapes were cultivated and the bubbly manufactured from the Champagne region of France? Well, I want you to forget this snobbish take on sparkling wines! Champagne is an eponym or an object that takes its name from a proper noun. Let's take the Adirondack chair, for example. Is an Adirondack chair only an Adirondack chair if the wood was cultivated and the chair manufactured in the Adirondack region of New York State? No. It's a style of chair named for where it originated. I realize this is an unpopular opinion and my inbox is going to be filled with arguments as to why I am wrong (which I will disregard, tee-hee).

Write about an unpopular opinion you hold. Do you think pizza is the devil's food? That *Hamilton* was the worst musical ever created? Or that mosquito bites are enjoyable? Now's the time to divulge.

October 27

Before my son was born, my partner and I kept his name a secret. My number one reason for doing this was not because I was afraid my other pregnant friends (and I had many who were pregnant at the same time as I was) might steal the name, but rather I didn't want to hear about the people our friends and relatives knew with that same name. "Oh, my friend's ex-boyfriend's name was Orion and he turned out to be a stalker." "Oh, my cousin-in-law's high school prom date was named Orion, and he kept his finger nail clippings in a coffee can next to his bed." I didn't want to hear the stories that may have convinced me to name my son something different.

Do you have a secret? Without writing about the secret itself, write about your reasons for keeping this secret.

October 28

Dada poetry or writing branched from the Dada art movement from the early 1900s tends to rely on mere chance as its creative mechanism to create nonsensical texts. A technique often used is cutting the words of a text out and then putting them all in a vessel of some kind (like a bag or hat) and selecting one at a time at random to compose a new text.

Ready to get out some scissors and glue? If you don't have art supplies at the ready, find a different way to create randomness. Perhaps you grab a book from your shelf and open to random pages and pick out a random word from each page. Maybe you send out a mass text and ask everyone to send you a single word. Get creative! The gold is found in the process and not in what you end up creating.

October 29

"Reclaimed language" is language that was historically used to target a person or group (like a slur or insult) that is then reappropriated by the intended target as a means of resilience and empowerment.

For example, whenever someone calls me a "b!tch" (or worse), I simply say, "Joke's on them because that's my favorite compliment." (And that's true!)

In recent years, there has also been a reclamation of the word "queer" in the LGBTQIA+ community. Historically used to emasculate and shame, in the 21st century we proudly cheer, "We're here, we're queer, and there's nothing you can do about it." I, myself, openly and unapologetically identify as a queer b!tch.

In today's writing, think of an insult that has been hurled at you and reclaim it.

October 30

For over a decade, famed painter and art instructor Bob Ross hosted the TV show, *The Joy of Painting*. During each episode, Bob demonstrated to viewers how to go from a blank canvas to creating a magical landscape using the wet-on-wet painting technique. He inspired and encouraged viewers, famously saying, "We don't make mistakes, we just have happy accidents."

Write about a time when a mistake was actually a happy accident.

October 31

Today is Halloween, but spooky movies and stories always, well, spook me! I'm not a fan of the horror genre. I can barely make my way through the movie *Hocus Pocus* even as a grown adult! I know! I'm a total wimp!

That is why I love artist Kelly Gilleran's re-imagining of traditional Halloween characters as pin-up girls. One illustration shows an oversized, wrinkled mummy face with an hourglass figure clad in a white, frilly dress. In another piece, a bloody, oversized skull is juxtaposed with a form-fitting skeleton bodysuit paired with some black heels and the character standing in a cutesy, feminine pose.

For me, the unexpected fashionista bodies render the scary faces more silly than scary.

Today, write about something traditionally scary, but neutralize it with something silly or unexpected.

November 1

One thing that irks me to no end is when drivers don't use their turn signals. It makes me wonder in what other areas of their lives they just refuse to communicate with others. What emotional wounds from childhood are they subconsciously trying to heal via entitlement, dominance, or thrill on the road?

Traffic model after traffic model indicates that negative driving behavior negatively impacts traffic flow for *everyone* including the tailgating a-hole weaving in and out of lanes without signaling.

Write about something that you feel negatively impacts individuals and society as a whole. What keeps everyone on the trajectory if it's so bad?

November 2

Growing up, I thought the lyrics to the traditional lullaby "Rock-a-bye, Baby" were rather morbid: *Rock a bye baby on the tree top, / When the wind blows the cradle will rock, / When the bough breaks the cradle will fall, / And down will come baby, cradle and all.*

How is that supposed to make a child feel safe to go to sleep at night?

Many legends exist for the song's origins including that the lyrics were translated from a Native American lullaby. Some tribes were known to hang babies in cradleboards from tree branches to allow the wind to gently sway the babes to sleep. The line about the bough breaking is a metaphor for the child growing up and eventually making their own life as an adult.

Write your own lullaby that references things you said, did, or liked as a child. Include a metaphor that represents how you grew into adulthood.

November 3

In Kayo Chingonyi's poem "The last night of my 20s" published on *Poetry International's* website, he begins the poem with, "Fitting that the day should dawn / in this most Lumsdenesque of Lumsdenesque contexts."

I didn't know what it meant either, but after looking it up, I learned that the term referred to the poet Roddy Lumsden, the same way someone might say "Freudian" or "Machiavellian" or "Napoleonic".

Today, write about the last night of your 20s. (Or if you are not that old yet, write about the last year of your last decade. The last year of your teens or, my gosh, the last year of your... single digit years?) Oh, and don't forget to reference a writer or artist or other person whose work you admire, using their name as an adjective.

November 4

Esther Perel is an author and psychotherapist who specializes in romantic and sexual relationships. In her book *Mating in Captivity*, she writes, "Today, we turn to one person to provide what an entire village once did... Is it any wonder that so many relationships crumble under the weight of it all?" In articles and interviews, she has asserted that "[l]ove is a verb, not a permanent state of enthusiasm."

Write about what love can look like if it is demonstrated despite a lack of enthusiasm.

November 5

Tardigrades are one of the most widespread and resilient creatures on the planet. Even though they can be found on mountain summits, in the depths of the sea, in rainforests, and even in the polar desert of Antarctica, you wouldn't easily know that since as adults they are only about 0.5mm long. These micro-animals have been known to survive not only extreme temperatures, but also starvation and dehydration, exposure to radiation, extremely high and low pressures, and they have even survived exposure to outer space!

Tune into your inner tardigrade, and write about something you survived.

November 6

Elsie Allcock was born in 1918 and spent her entire life—over one hundred years—in the two-bedroom property in Huthwaite, Nottinghamshire, United Kingdom that she grew up in. Originally the home had no electricity or running water. During her time there, besides witnessing the many technological and infrastructure upgrades to her home and community, Elsie witnessed the ends of World War I and World War II and the terms of twenty-two British prime ministers.

Imagine living in the same home for over a century. Write about the changes you would witness over the span of that time. What changes would the home witness in you?

November 7

Author and academic Arthur Brooks often writes about the psychology of happiness. He believes to have happiness, you must also have unhappiness; to have joy, you must also have pain. "The pursuit of happiness isn't about eliminating discomfort," he wrote in a social media post. "It's about understanding that moments of suffering are inseparable from a meaningful life... When we numb ourselves to avoid negative feelings we inadvertently block the positive ones too. A full life demands openness to both."

Write about a time of sadness or pain that brought meaning to your life.

November 8

In Kevin Young's poem, "Ode to the Midwest" first published in *Poetry*, he manages to both poke fun at the region he grew up in and express his love for it. "I want to be doused / in cheese // & fried," he writes. "I want to write / a check in the express lane... I wanta drive // two blocks. Why walk". (I also love his use of the word "wanta" and the way we sometimes fall back into the accent and dialect of our home region when we are home or around others from the same area.)

Write about your hometown or region by writing a list of all the things you want to (or wanta) do or experience that can only be done in your area.

November 9

Rudolf Karel was a renowned Czech composer of the 20th century. During WWII, after the Nazis invaded, he joined the Czech resistance, but was arrested and tortured in Pankrác prison. While in prison, he continued composing despite having no instruments. He composed his five-act fairytale opera *Three Hairs of the Wise Old Man* with toilet paper and charcoal, using only his imagination to put the whole thing together. The 240 sheets he wrote on were smuggled out of the prison by a sympathetic officer. Unfortunately, he never lived to hear his masterpiece, dying while in another prison in Theresienstadt after he was forced to stand outside in freezing temperatures while suffering from dysentery and pneumonia.

Let Rudolf's dedication to his craft despite his dire conditions and circumstances inspire you today. Imagine a fairytale story, but don't write it out. For now, just imagine it. Watch the entire story play out in your mind before putting anything to paper.

November 10

Though he is mostly known as a renowned French poet of the late 1800s, Arthur Rimbaud, wrote all of his notable works as a teenager and young adult, retiring as a writer completely at age 21. In the second half of his life, he traveled the world and worked many different jobs before his untimely death at age 37 from bone cancer.

Write about your teenage years. How are you different or the same as you were in adolescence? How did you spend your time? How do you wish you spent your time? If you had achieved your greatest feats before age 21, what would they have been?

November 11

In China, November 11th is Singles' Day, an unofficial social holiday that celebrates being single. On this day, singles treat themselves similarly to how couples celebrate one another on Valentine's Day: treats, flowers, gifts, dinners out, and more. It is the world's largest shopping day, overshadowing even the United States' Black Friday and Cyber Monday events.

Whether you are single or not, write about how you could treat yourself if you took yourself out on a date. Would you buy yourself flowers or candy? Where would you take yourself out? Bonus points for actually doing it!

November 12

An Aeolian harp, named after the Greek god of wind, Aeolus, is a string instrument designed to elicit sound when the wind passes across it.

Today, I invite you to become a human Aeolian harp. Place yourself outside, near an open window or door, or even near an air vent. Close your eyes and feel the breeze as it crosses your body. Maybe it's a particularly windy day, maybe the air currents are more subtle. Imagine the breeze generating whatever ideas coming to mind. Write them down.

November 13

Jalaluddin Rumi was a poet who lived in the 13th century in what is now Afghanistan and Tajikistan. One of his most famous poems, "The Guest House," compares a human being to a guest house for emotions and experiences, advising the reader to welcome each like they would welcome a visitor in their home. In a translation by Coleman Barks, Rumi writes, "Even if they're a crowd of sorrows, / who violently sweep your house / empty of its furniture, / still, treat each guest honorably... The dark thought, the shame, the malice, / meet them at the door laughing, / and invite them in."

Today, write about your emotions as if they are unexpected visitors to your home. How does each behave when they arrive? What brought them there? How would you interact with them during their stay? When and how do they leave?

November 14

Suely Cassiano is a Brazilian-American artist who has created breathtaking landscapes from all over the US: the Statue of Liberty in New York Harbor, the Golden Gate Bridge, Bell Rock in Arizona, Key West Beach, and more. In one painting that stood out as very different from the rest of her works, a nude woman lay prone with monarch butterfly wings sprouting from her back.

Write about a human who has the physical features of another animal. Maybe a human has monarch wings on their back like in Cassiano's painting, maybe they have the neck of a giraffe, the mane of a lion, the hooves of a deer, the ears of an elephant, or the stripes of a zebra. Maybe they have the rough tongue of a house cat, talons like an eagle, or the shell of a turtle. How is their life impacted if they live in a world of humans not like them?

November 15

In his book *Peace Is Every Step*, Vietnamese, Buddhist monk, peace activist, and author Thích Nhất Hạnh wrote, "Hope is important because it can make the present moment less difficult to bear. If we believe that tomorrow will be better, we can bear a hardship today."

Write about your hopes for the future. How does your hope help you get through the hard times?

November 16

In her chapbook *Dialogue With the Dead*, poet Danielle Badra composes contrapuntal poems (poems written in two columns that can be read both individually and together as one larger poem) from her sister's poetry she discovered after her sister passed away from a genetic heart condition at age 28 that no one knew she had.

In a podcast interview with Tyler Greene of This Is My Family, she said of writing these poems, "I felt like I was communing with [my sister]... it did not feel like she wasn't there. It felt like she was there, and I was talking to her."

Today, write in conversation with a piece of writing written by a loved one—a poem, an email, a social media post, a text, anything.

November 17

In her book *The Gifts of Imperfection*, best-selling self-help author, Brené Brown, refers to herself as "a recovering perfectionist and an aspiring good-enoughist." She believes that perfectionism is rooted in a fear of shame, blame, and pain, and being able to accept a more effective, comfortable, and graceful outcome or result leads to greater happiness, less stress, and more self-compassion.

Write about how you might replace "100% perfect" with "good enough" in one (or more!) aspect(s) of your life.

November 18

If you've ever read a textbook or scientific paper in your lifetime, you have probably seen a footnote, text written at the bottom of a page marked by a superscript number, asterisk, or other symbol that usually includes a deeper explanation, background information necessary to understand the main text, and/or a citation.

Footnotes can also be used creatively in poetry or prose to add depth, complexity, and/or humor like when a character in a play or movie breaks the fourth wall to talk to the audience.

In Layli Long Soldier's poem "Urning," the footnotes themselves become their own kind of poem.

In today's writing, use at least three footnotes. Use them to provide unique definitions of words, provide meaningful context, and/or make a joke.

November 19

Chloe Flower is an American composer famed for blending classical style piano together with pop, rap, and R & B. She calls her style "popsical," and her unique blend has garnered her fame and accolades having performed on widely-viewed stages such as the Grammys and Oscars.

Write in a way that blends two seemingly opposing genres or styles. Historical fiction meets space opera? A murder mystery for children? Erotica written in verse?

November 20

Parasites are absolutely terrifying; so many are involved with brain manipulation of their hosts. For example, the green-banded broodsac is a flatworm that infects snails. It takes over the snail's eyestalks, causing them to swell and change color so they look more like a caterpillar. They also compel the snails to move to less protected areas where they could be more easily seen by birds. Why? Because the parasites reproduce *inside birds*. Then their eggs are released into the world via the bird's feces. The only way the parasites can get to the birds, though, is if they get into the snails first. And think, the snails probably don't realize their minds are being controlled by parasites. They just think, "Oh wow, that wide open sunny spot looks nice, I'll go slime my way over there." And then BAM! Bird breakfast.

Write from the perspective of a parasite that needs to reach its host. What lengths will it go just to reproduce?

November 21

Amy Ringholz is a Wyoming-based visual artist who has built a career creating vibrant, colorful portraits of the American Mountain West's fauna. Bears, wolves, moose, rabbits, owls and more appear not in their customary gray and brown earth tones, but rather in a rainbow kaleidoscope of colors, as if appearing from a dream world.

Whether true or completely made up, write about a technicolor animal that appears in a dream.

November 22

A speech delay that prevented her from speaking until age four and a literacy delay that kept her from reading until age seven didn't hold back Nigerian-American spoken-word poet, artist, filmmaker, educator, and journalist, Amanda Eke. In fact, the title of her podcast and TV show *The Poet Speaks* is a nod to her younger self. Now, as an adult, she travels the world and connects with locals to learn about the oral storytelling and spoken-word traditions that shape people and their cultures.

Write about something that took you a while to learn as a child. How did this struggle impact you then? How does it still impact you today, if it does at all?

November 23

The Fermi Paradox asks if it has been billions of years since the Big Bang and if trillions upon trillions of celestial bodies exist, why haven't researchers been able to detect any signs of intelligent life beyond our planet?

In today's writing, take a crack at answering this paradox. No need to do any special research if you don't want to. You could come at the question earnestly, or write a ridiculous answer. Up to you!

November 24

In her powerful poem "Why I Hate Raisins," poet Natalie Diaz surprisingly starts her poem off with a definition of love: "Love is a pound of sticky raisins / packed tight in black and white / government boxes the day we had no / groceries." The poem goes on to recount a story of a little kid with a stomachache after devouring the whole pound of raisins herself, and, not understanding the dynamics of poverty as a child, complains to her mother that she wants to be able to eat a sandwich like other kids. At the end of the poem, the speaker recounts how she still hates raisins because "now I know /my mom was hungry that day, too, / and I ate all the raisins."

Write the back story about why you hate a certain food or something else—a particular day, a particular item of clothing, a particular word, whatever calls to you.

November 25

In regards to writer's block, slam poet Christian "Soul Stuf" Perfas wrote, "[W]hen I can't seem to write, I listen. I dip into spaces where poets congregate and see if I can pick up a gem or two from what they decide to share. [Fellow slam poet Antonio Cortez Appling] used to call this 'collecting artifacts.'"

Today, collect some artifacts before sitting down to write. Read and listen to the words of writers you admire and those you have just learned about. Sit and take in art from artists you admire and those you have just learned about. Listen to music from musicians that you admire and those you have just learned about. But don't forget to take notes! What did you enjoy about these people's work? What words did they use that intrigued you? What moods did they convey that you also want to convey? What subjects or themes inspired you?

November 26

People who live with prosopagnosia struggle to recognize other people's faces. The condition is also known as "face-blindness". An estimated 2.5% of the population lives with this condition. People with prosopagnosia often rely on other context clues to help them identify a person such as where they are located, their gait, their hairstyle, or what they're wearing.

Today, describe a person in your life by attributes other than their facial appearance. What is unique about the way they walk, dress, style their hair, or where they can be found in the world?

November 27

A trip wire is a kind of booby trap that when triggered sets off an alarm, opens a trap door, or sets off a weapon like a landmine. A metaphorical trip wire is a kind of ultimatum, typically a deadline paired with a condition that then triggers an action, which can be helpful when struggling with procrastination or grappling with a decision. For example, "If my manuscript hasn't been picked up by an agent or publisher by December 31st, I'm going to self-publish it." The tripwire is not just the date itself, but also the condition that the manuscript hasn't been selected by that time. Another example is, "If I don't use my Peloton even one time in the next month, I'm going to sell it," or "If my current romantic partner doesn't show interest in taking the next step in the relationship by the holidays, I'm going to break up with them."

Have you been putting off taking action on something? Write about the situation and see how setting a trip wire influences your thoughts or feelings.

November 28

Some of Holly Osburn's whimsical paintings look like they came straight from a Beatrix Potter-esque fairytale: ground squirrels hanging laundry to dry, a lost mouse holding a lantern atop directional signs, an aproned hedgehog stirring tea in a cup that's as big as it is, a toadstool house covered in snow, and more.

Taking inspiration from the world of fairytales and make-believe, include some anthropomorphic animals (animals that are depicted as behaving like humans) in your writing today.

November 29

Disposable diapers are one of the biggest contributors to landfill waste in the United States, with the country discarding millions of tons of diapers each year. Because each diaper takes hundreds of years to break down, the very first one ever dumped in is still out in a dump somewhere.

A Texas-based company aims to mitigate this waste by selling diapers paired with packets of *Pestalotiopsis microspora*, a fungi that feeds on and breaks down plastic. When a diaper gets changed, caregivers place one packet inside the dirty diaper before throwing it away. After nine months, the fungi will have rendered the diaper into soil.

The company's goal is to eventually expand to include adult diapers and menstrual products too.

Today, write about or reference mushrooms, fungi, molds, yeast, and/or mildew.

November 30

Rachel Anne Accurso, better known as the American YouTube sensation Ms. Rachel, built her career creating online content focused on supporting young children in their language development. She then expanded into books, appearances, collaborations, original music, a deal with Netflix and more.

She faced severe backlash for many reasons including wishing viewers a happy Pride month and having a nonbinary collaborator on her show. But she received the most online aggression after voicing her support for children around the world suffering due to war, particularly children living and dying in Palestine.

In response to the criticism, she said, "I wouldn't be Ms. Rachel if I didn't deeply care about all kids... and I will risk my career over and over to stand up for them."

Write about what is so important to you that you would risk everything for it.

December 1

By fighting and winning against colonization, Ethiopia has maintained most if not all of their own cultural traditions. For example, Ethiopia has its own script known as ግዕዝ or Geʿez when written in the Roman alphabet. Ethiopia has its own calendar that is eight years behind the Gregorian calendar most of the rest of the world is accustomed to. The Ethiopian calendar has twelve months all with thirty days followed by a thirteenth month with far fewer days that acts as a kind of leap week. Ethiopia even has its own way of keeping hourly time. For them, a new day starts at dawn rather than at midnight. Because Ethiopia is located close to the equator, the number of daylight hours does not shift very much throughout the year like it does in other places like Alaska, France, New Zealand, or South Africa.

Write about an aspect of your culture—such as the writing system or method for telling time—that you wish you could adjust. What just doesn't make sense to you?

December 2

Whether you follow astrology or not, you might be familiar with the concept of the twelve zodiac signs: Aries, Taurus, Gemini, Cancer, Leo, Virgo, Libra, Scorpio, Sagittarius, Capricorn, Aquarius, and Pisces. Some astrologers, however, posit there is a thirteenth zodiac sign: Ophiuchus, or the serpent bearer. This constellation sits behind the sun from approximately November 29 to December 18. Ophiuchans are believed to be influenced by Pluto, and because the constellation is associated with Asclepius, a great healer in Greek mythology, those with strong Ophiuchus influence might be drawn to medical and healing professions.

Write from the perspective of a healer. Whom do you want to heal, and from what?

December 3

As glaciers move, they create sounds that can indicate how the air and water within and beneath them are moving. For example, "ice sizzle" is a sound akin to the fizzing of carbonated drinks that occurs when trapped air bubbles are released as a glacier melts. "Ice quakes" are cracking sounds caused by fractures within glacial ice. "Moulins" are a kind of roar created when water moves through vertical passages within a glacier. A glacier might groan when the ice expands or contracts with the changing of temperature. All of these sounds (and there are even more not mentioned here) collectively are called a glacier's "voice" or "song."

Write from the perspective of a glacier. What would they want to sing about? What would the lyrics of their song be?

December 4

When I was little, I thought the expression "to make ends meet" was "to make *end's meat.*" I thought that if someone "couldn't make end's meat" that they had so little money they couldn't even afford the end cut of meat (usually the smallest and least desirable piece of meat). Or if they *could* make end's meat that they still didn't have a lot of money, but at least they could earn the end cut of meat.

Write about something that you failed to understand correctly and how you figured out you had made a mistake.

December 5

Hygge (pronounced HOO-guh), is a set of cultural practices derived from Denmark and Norway that essentially puts an emphasis on comfort, warmth, and conviviality. I have heard it referred to as "cozy core": bulky sweaters, sitting by a fire, hot cocoa, feel-good novels, anything that evokes *coziness*.

Today before you start writing, get *cozy*. If it's not sweater weather, put on a cozy t-shirt and some cozy shorts. Pick out a cozy beverage. Sit in a cozy spot. Think cozy thoughts. Then, write some cozy writing.

December 6

Andrés Sánchez is a queer/trans Mexican poet who migrated to the US at age five. Their full-length collection of poetry, *This Body*, debuted in December 2021. About their book, they wrote, "What started as a book about heartbreak became something more—a journey of self-love and reclaiming my identity. *This Body* turned into an anthem, a way to reconcile past mistakes and imagine a brighter path forward. It was a moment to forgive myself and finally leave the past where it belongs."

Today, write about heartbreak. As the writing progresses, imagine what a brighter path forward looks like and incorporate that vision into the writing.

December 7

Pattie Gonia is a drag queen and environmental activist. In her TED Talk "Why joy is a serious way to take action" she argued that "[T]he problem in the climate movement isn't just the abundance of carbon, it is the lack of joy. The scientific facts, the doom and gloom, they scare people... But joy... is strategic... joy inspires momentum... Do not underestimate the power of joy." She said, "[I]f there's one thing I have learned from the art form of drag, it's that you can take fighting for something seriously without taking yourself too seriously."

Write about the area of your life that could use more joy. What would this area look like if it were somehow infused with drag?

December 8

Titus Kaphar is a renowned American artist known for his artistic "amending" of historical paintings and sculptures, like with his famous work "Behind the Myth of Benevolence".

On his website, he writes that he "cuts, crumples, shrouds, shreds, stitches, tars, twists, binds, erases, breaks, tears, and turns the paintings and sculptures he creates" with the aim of revealing "something of what has been lost and to investigate the power of a rewritten history."

Either using personal writing about your own history or another text depicting the history of your country, region, or community, use Kaphar's methods (either literally or figuratively) of cutting, crumpling, shrouding, shredding, etc. to rewrite history and/or reveal something new.

December 9

In her poem "How to Write a Poem in a Time of War," first published in *Poetry*, former Poet Laureate of the United States, Joy Harjo begins the piece in italics with the sentence, *"You can't begin just anywhere."* The poem changes to roman font and describes the many despairs and all the ugliness war causes and leaves behind. Then the italics appear again, as if a higher power is correcting the poet herself, *"No, start here. Deer peer from the edge / of the woods."* The poem continues with imagery of Native Americans being ripped from their families and communities by white colonizers. The last section of the poem then describes the scene of a grandfather embedding his grandchildren's hearts with a song that the white soldiers wouldn't be able to see or take away from them and that would help them to return home someday. That is when the italics appear for the final time instructing the reader to "Begin here." (Read the full poem in the bonus materials.)

Begin today's writing with a call to return home.

December 10

In her short life, dying at only age 36, Augusta Ada King, Countess of Lovelace aka Ada Lovelace was a mathematician who worked with fellow mathematician Charles Babbage in theorizing complicated "analytical engines"—the precursors to computers as we know them. Lovelace proposed the possibility of "encoding" information outside of mere calculation. Whereas her counterparts were focused mainly on devising machines to perform arithmetic and solve equations, Lovelace saw the future of computers as being intertwined and collaborative with human life.

As a girl, her mother encouraged Lovelace's interest in mathematics hoping she wouldn't turn out like her father, poet Lord Byron, who had had multiple affairs and was the biological father of children born as a result. Lady Caroline Lamb, one of his lovers, described him as "mad, bad, and dangerous to know."

Write about whether or not the people who raised you supported your interests. How did that impact who you are today?

December 11

In her poem "How Delicious to Say It," poet Vievee Francis uses italics to emphasize different words throughout the poem, presumably the ones that are "delicious" to say, words like "*loquacious, Liebchen, Schätzchen.*"

In the final lines, she writes, "Your name spun through the reel, wound up from the bass / of me. How I want to say it, and hear my own, again. // for Matthew".

Though written as a simple dedication, the build up of the poem indicates that the speaker's favorite word of all is the name Matthew, which is her husband's name.

Make a list of words that are "delicious" to say in your opinion. Try to come up with at least ten, and then try to use all of the words in your writing today.

December 12

In his book *The Greatest Miracle in the World,* American author, Og Mandino, wrote, "Beginning today, treat everyone you meet as if they were going to be dead by midnight. Extend them all the care, kindness and understanding you can muster. Your life will never be the same again."

Write how you would behave differently if you knew someone you deeply love was going to die today. Write about how you would behave differently if you knew an acquaintance was going to die today. Write about how you would behave differently if someone you dislike was going to die today. Write about how you would behave differently if someone you despise was going to die today.

December 13

My grandmother Marie died on this day in 2002. Seventeen years later to the day, my father was rushed to the hospital with sepsis and pneumonia on top of his stage 4 lung cancer. That evening, while my mother stayed at the hospital with him, I returned to their house to walk and feed the dogs. On the walk, an owl swooped over my head. I didn't even hear it. I only felt the whoosh of the bird's wings before watching it fly away into the sunset sky. I just knew it was my grandmother telling me that she was there with us.

Write about your ancestors. Do you ever feel like you commune with them from the other side? Have they sent you signs? Even if it not, or if you don't believe in such things, imagine what kind of sign a deceased loved one might try to send you if they could and why.

December 14

Author of *Living in Five Senses,* Gretchen Rubin, theorizes that each person has what she calls a "neglected sense," or one of our big five senses (sight, sound, taste, smell, and touch) that we pay less attention to, a sense that we rarely turn to for pleasure or comfort. She believes identifying your neglected sense could benefit your life, and open your world to new experiences. For example, if someone's neglected sense is smell, they might try amplifying their olfactory experiences by adding scented candles to their decor, buying a new perfume, or paying closer attention to the aromas of their dinner.

I believe identifying your neglected sense could improve your writing as well because your descriptions of people, places, or objects could be enhanced by making sure to include details that may ordinarily be left out.

Revisit a piece of writing. How might honing in on a particular sense change how a character, setting, or prop is portrayed?

December 15

Hippopotamuses are native to sub-Saharan Africa as well as the Nile river. The word "hippopotamus" derived from the ancient Greek "hippo" which translates to "horse" and "potamos" which translates to "river."

Even though they're considered a land mammal, hippos have extraordinary underwater capabilities. Besides being able to close their nostrils and ears to keep water out, they have an innate reflex that allows them to rise to the surface for air while they sleep! No need to interrupt their sweet dreams just to take a breath!

Write about what you wish you could accomplish in your sleeping hours.

December 16

In his poem "Just Maybe", poet and minister Chidube Nkiruka wrote that love would "hurt a little / But if it didn't hurt a little, maybe it wouldn't be love / Maybe we can't love / at a distance / if we are going to love / with our presence".

Write about why love might "hurt a little".

December 17

In the epic poem *The Odyssey*, sirens are described as female human-like creatures whose songs entrance sailors and lure them to their deaths. To be able to hear the sirens' song and still survive, Odysseus directs his crew members to plug their ears with beeswax and to tie him to the mast of the ship and not release him even if he begs them to. Unable to hear the sirens' song, the crew navigates their ship past the island where the sirens live, and Odysseus is able to hear the enchanting yet deadly song and live to tell the tale.

Write about a temptation that you know is not good for you. How are you able to resist?

December 18

In 2002, painting instructor, Wendy Lovoy, prompted her students to BYOB to her painting classes so they would feel more relaxed, less critical of themselves, and just get out of their own heads. Her idea sparked what now is referred to "Paint & Sip" nights popular at bars, restaurants, and other venues where a professional artist comes and instructs participants, step by step, on creating a simple painting that they can then take home with them, all while they enjoy whatever libations suit them best.

For this writing prompt, I encourage you to BYOB—alcohol not required! You can bring your own coffee, lemonade, mocktail, or other special drink. Try to make it something you don't usually have—a treat! When you take your first sip, notice all of your senses: what it looks like in its vessel, what it sounds like pouring, what you sound like sipping it, what it smells like as you pull your cup or glass to your mouth, what the temperature is, and then finally what it tastes like. Does this beverage invoke any memories?

December 19

Anansi (also written as Ananse) is often depicted in West African folklore as a spider and is known to be a trickster, using his cleverness and creativity to outsmart and out-maneuver stronger opponents. However, sometimes his trickery backfires on him.

In one tale, he tries to hoard all the knowledge in the world in a pot, keeping it for himself. To keep the pot of knowledge away from others, he tries to hide it in a tree, but keeps falling each time he tries to climb while holding the pot in his arms. When his son sees him and teases him for not strapping the pot to his back instead of trying to carry it in his arms, Anansi gets so angry that he shatters the pot on the ground, spreading the wisdom all over the world, which is why wisdom still exists everywhere across the globe today.

Write about a time something backfired on you. What were you hoping to accomplish? What happened instead?

December 20

Professional basketball player Kobi Simmons is credited with the quote, "A bottle of water can be 50 cents at a supermarket, $2 at the gym, $3 at the movies, and $6 on a plane. Same water. Only thing that changed its value was the place. So the next time you feel your worth is nothing, maybe you're at the wrong place." (Man, those prices seem kinda cheap, right? Inflation is wild!)

Write about the places where you feel like your worth is acknowledged and appreciated.

December 21

In Shakeema Smalls' prose poem, "I know I been changed" first published in *The Indianapolis Review,* the speaker envisions what will happen after she has passed away: "I'll leave no children and no lovers... Maybe I'll leave a fur coat to a beloved friend. A box of tools to a dutiful neighbor... They will discuss how expensive my things are, how rare a life." The speaker also recounts the instructions she left behind: "I told them to burn me... Cover my breasts in milk and flowers like spring. Let the possums admire my silver gown."

Write the instructions you want to leave behind for your loved ones. What do you want to leave behind and to whom? What might your loved ones say to each other while going through your belongings?

December 22

Serotinous plants are species whose seeds stay within their cones or fruits for extended periods of time, sometimes even years! The adaptive benefit is particularly significant in fire-prone environments. In fact, it's usually a fire itself that spurs the seeds to open, letting them take advantage of a clear landscape without competition for sun or nutrients from other plants.

Write about a time when a serious stressor spurred you into action.

December 23

In KC Davis' book *How to Keep House While Drowning*, she breaks down the sometimes Goliath task of tidying up in her "5 Things Method". She theorizes most tidying up can be categorized into trash, dishes, laundry, things with a designated place, and things without a designated place. She suggests focusing on one category at a time, even if that means completing each category over a span of time instead of all at once.

Playing off of Davis' method, I suggest the "5 Things Method" for quick editing. 1. Review a piece of writing and remove adverbs; a word ending in -ly like *really, quietly, suddenly, finally, literally, nicely*, etc. 2. Remove or replace adjectives like *beautiful, big*, or any color recognizable by a toddler. 3. Look for opportunities to remove the word "that". 4. Delete the phrase "started to". 5. Replace any combination of phrases like "I/he/she/they/it was/saw/watched/heard/felt/smelled" etc. with a stronger verb.

December 24

My mom is a very talented knitter, crocheter, and cross-stitcher. She can make *anything*. I can even send her a picture of an item I'd like to have, and now that she's retired with nothing else better to do, she'll figure out how to make it for me. I am blessed to have many blankets she hand made to my exact specifications among other items: a star-shaped bunting for my son, the same gray cowl/vest Jennifer Lawrence sports in the Hunger Games movie, a remake of my childhood mittens my grandmother had knit —one red, one green, with "Stop" and "Go" stitched into the palms.

While on the phone with my mom one time, she said "If I could just knit and watch TV all day, I would be so happy." And I said, "Isn't that what you do already?" And after a brief pause she said, "Yeah, I guess I'm so happy then."

Write about how you wish you could spend your time. How would you know whether or not you were so happy?

December 25

Long, long ago when I was a high school foreign exchange student, my then-boyfriend and I stayed together despite the long distance. This is long before social media or Zoom, and Skype was in its nascence and not well-known yet. We used long-distance phone cards to be able to talk on the phone for twenty minutes once a month or so.

One time when he sent me a present in the mail, I opened the package and found multiple CDs labeled "The Lion, The Witch, and The Wardrobe." When I put the first CD in my CD player, I wept. It was his voice. With no smartphones like we have now that allow us to easily record our voices whenever we want, he recorded himself using equipment one of his friend's dad's owned.

Write about the most romantic or thoughtful gift you ever received.

December 26

Archbishop Desmond Tutu was a South African theologian, author, and anti-apartheid and human rights activist who deeply believed in the power of forgiveness. His book *The Book of Forgiving: The Fourfold Path for Healing Ourselves and Our World* that he co-authored with his daughter, Rev. Mpho A. Tutu taught me that forgiving doesn't have to equate to keeping someone in my life and pretending like they never hurt me. I can forgive someone, and not wish revenge upon them, and not seethe with anger and resentment when I think about them, and then still choose to "release" that relationship (as it is put in the book) instead of renewing it. That realization and that "permission" helped me heal a lot of past wounds.

Write about a situation in which you forgave someone or asked for forgiveness. Was that relationship restored and renewed? Or was that relationship still released?

December 27

I need to tell you about Florin. He worked at a grocery store self-checkout in Wyoming, and he wasn't just superficially friendly as most people in customer service are, genuine care radiated from him. While checking out at the grocery store after I learned of my father's cancer diagnosis, Florin came up to me and asked if I was okay. I wept in front of him, telling him my news. He hugged me and said, "I will pray. I will pray."

He was even featured in the local newspaper, just for being a nice guy. The headline read, "Florin brings calm to self-checkout line". When he announced he and his family were moving back to Romania, I wasn't the only one who felt shocked and saddened. Before he left, another article was written about him and his impact on our community. "Thank you, Florin: Florin and family are leaving after 15 years of bringing joy".

Write about a hometown hero. Someone who might go under the radar, but who deserves recognition.

December 28

Grammy award-winning singer-songwriter John Legend has a unique approach to songwriting. He says, "Some people start with the lyrics first because they know what they want to talk about... but for me the music tells me what to talk about."

Today, instead of writing from a prompt, let the page tell you "what to talk about".

December 29

Marathons are 26.2 miles (42.165 kilometers) long and ultra-marathons vary in length anywhere from 30 miles to 100 miles, and the longest certified race (as of this writing) is 3,100 miles long! A study published in *BMC Medicine* showed that runners of long-distance races like these lose up to 6% of their brain mass during their events!

Write for 26.2 minutes (that is 26 minutes and 12 seconds) or longer if you want to do an ultra-marathon of writing! Don't go back and edit, just write for the full length of time. At the end, set a goal to cut 6% of the words. If you write on a computer, it'll be easy to take a word count and decrease it by 6%. If you handwrite, it's a little trickier, but you can do it by page or lines on your paper. Give it a shot!

December 30

It's New Year's Eve Eve! Remember when you wrote something "halfway" on July 2nd, "Halfway Day"? Return to that piece of writing and complete it now with six months worth of new insights, experiences, and ideas to draw from.

December 31

Ah! December 31st, the last day of the year, and also my little cousin Cindy's birthday. Happy birthday, Cindy!

But you know what? Time is just made up. Days, months, years, they're all just fabricated by people in power and kept in place because of societal convention.

The oldest known New Year festival dates back to 2000 BCE in Mesopotamia. The new year was celebrated on the first new moon after the vernal equinox, which would be around April of our current calendar. The early Roman calendar used to begin March 1st. Egypt's Alexandrian calendar (also known as the Coptic calendar) started on what would the equivalent of August 29th .

So really this "end" is more of a *symbol* of an end because what is time anyway?

Write about time and ends and end times.

About the Author

Anne Marie Wells is an award-winning poet, playwright, memoirist, and oral storyteller. She is the founder of The Joy of Poeting, and author of two collections of poetry: *Survived By: A Memoir in Verse + Other Poems* (Curious Corvid Publishing, 2023) and *Mother, (v)* which won the 2023 Cinnamon Press Chapbook Contest and debuted in 2024. She also authored two children's books: *Mommy, Why Am I a Bird?* (Imprensa Universidade de Coimbra, 2015) and *Underwater Explorers & Rescuers* (Ethical Seafood Research Publishing, 2025).

She is a certified listener poet through The Good Listening Project and earned a certificate in social emotional arts through The Arts & Healing Initiative. She is the content and copy editor for Mama's Kitchen Press and works as a freelance copy editor, ghostwriter, grant writer, writing coach, and creative writing instructor. When she's not writing, she's reading a book for one of her many book clubs, enjoying long walks in the outdoors with her family, completing *The New York Times* crossword puzzle, or doggy paddling in the shallow end of the public pool.

Learn more at AnneMarieWellsWriter.com.